Practical Wisd...

"David and Walter have written the guide I want every parent to follow and every youth pastor to be able to give to parents. Teenagers are formed best when parents and youth leaders are partners, and this guide offers the practical roadmap churches need to make that possible."

—**Kara Powell,** PhD; executive director, Fuller Youth Institute; chief of leadership formation, Fuller Seminary; coauthor of *3 Big Questions That Change Every Teenager*

"Dr. Walter Surdacki and Dr. David Fraze are absolute *giants* in the world of youth ministry. There is no youth ministry tag team more gifted, qualified, and prepared to educate and equip parents or youth ministers for the task of raising adolescents to a living faith in the living God."

—**David Rubio,** youth minister imagineer, aspiring firebender, emotional decathlete, Otter Creek Church

"What does it mean to be a good parent? What does it mean to lead a good youth ministry? On their own, these are important questions. But such questions shouldn't be left 'on their own.' It just so happens that there is less and less of a link between these questions; they are more and more left to be answered without connection. What makes for a 'good parent' by our middle-class measures may have less to do with supporting and seeking support from a congregational youth ministry. However, to bring these questions back together, to place the hand of the parent back in the hand of the youth pastor will take much more than creativity or charisma. It will necessitate wisdom. Wisdom—unlike creativity and charisma—is never self-created but comes only from placing yourself in conversation with others already down the road. This is just what *Practical Wisdom for Youth Group Parents* provides. It's an invitation to walk with Walter and David, seeing and learning the ways of wisdom. It will be worth every minute."

—**Andrew Root,** professor of youth and family ministry, Luther Seminary; author of *The End of Youth Ministry?*

"*Practical Wisdom for Youth Group Parents* is a great follow-up to Fraze's *Practical Wisdom for Youth Ministry*. There was a time in youth ministry when we took teens away from their parents, thinking we could spiritually form them better. As Surdacki points out, 'What we did didn't work.' In teaching youth ministry at Oklahoma Christian University, partnering with parents is core content in one of my foundational classes. This new book will be an excellent addition to that content for my students. The biblical emphasis in the book is dead on. The practical wisdom comes from years of experience. The conclusion and the forms in the back are also very practical and informative. Church leaders would be wise to check this out."

—**Dudley Chancey,** PhD; professor of ministry, director of the
   Intergenerational Faith Center, Oklahoma Christian University

"Parents are an invaluable resource to youth ministries in our churches. This truth is driven home in *Practical Wisdom for Youth Group Parents*. Fraze and Surdacki bring a wealth of experience to the subject as they give attainable, practical steps any parent can take to partner with their youth minister. My son recently began his career as a youth minister. I would love for the parents at his church to have this resource. It would be a first step to a great partnership where their teens' faith would be strengthened."

—**Chris Hatchett,** SLK campus minister

"For parents who want to support their church's youth ministry but struggle with the 'how,' this book is a desperately needed resource. Drawing on their experience as youth ministers as well as parents of teens, David Fraze and Walter Surdacki offer a wealth of practical suggestions for partnering with your youth minister—from offering much-needed support and encouragement to handling conflict with integrity and compassion. I would love to see parents and youth leadership teams read this book together, letting it spark important conversations about youth ministry and further ideas for partnership."

—**Lauren Calvin Cooke,** PhD candidate in religious education,
   Emory University

"Some books are written for youth ministers. Some are written for parents of teens. Others are for teens. *Practical Wisdom for Youth Group Parents* is for all of them. This is one of the most helpful, practical, hopeful books you will find on healthy student ministry. Dr. Fraze and Dr. Surdacki combine years of wisdom, experience, success, and failure to provide a book that will strengthen youth ministers and youth ministries for years to come."

> —**Josh Ross,** lead minister, Sycamore View Church, Memphis; author of *Re\entry*

"Any wise and experienced youth worker knows that trying to do youth ministry without partnering with families is like trying to nurture flowers without regard for the soil from which they grow. What we have in this book is truly practical wisdom from two veteran youth workers, both widely recognized for their wisdom and experience! They've seen the benefits of what I call 'trans-parent' youth ministry, and they've managed in this book to give parents a readable guide for how to maximize and steward their teenager's youth group experience. If I were a youth pastor, I would give this book to every parent of every student in my youth group. And if I were the parent of a teenager *in* a youth group, I'd be an eager reader! This is a book we've needed!"

> —**Dr. Duffy Robbins,** professor of Christian ministry, Grove City College, Grove City, PA

"If parents will give this book a chance, you will understand the world of a youth minister. This helps parents understand that the church and the family are two divine designs of God that are truly powerful when they work together. This book is rich with theory but also practical advice for youth ministers and parents. This book is a difference-maker."

> —**Robert Oglesby,** director, Center for Youth and Family Ministry; instructor, Department of Bible, Missions and Ministry, Abilene Christian University

PRACTICAL WISDOM

FOR
YOUTH GROUP PARENTS

PRACTICAL WISDOM

FOR
YOUTH GROUP PARENTS

PARTNERING WITH YOUR YOUTH MINISTER

DR. DAVID FRAZE
Lubbock Christian University

DR. WALTER SURDACKI
Lipscomb University

LEAFWOOD
PUBLISHERS
an imprint of Abilene Christian University Press

PRACTICAL WISDOM FOR YOUTH GROUP PARENTS
Partnering with Your Youth Minister

LEAFWOOD
PUBLISHERS
an imprint of Abilene Christian University Press

Copyright © 2022 by David Fraze and Walter Surdacki

ISBN 978-1-68426-411-7

Printed in the United States of America

Cataloging-in-Publication Data is on file at the Library of Congress, Washington, DC.

Cover design by ThinkPen Design, LLC
Series interior text design by Sandy Armstrong, Strong Design
Typeset by Scribe Inc.

Leafwood Publishers is an imprint of Abilene Christian University Press
ACU Box 29138
Abilene, Texas 79699
1-877-816-4455
www.leafwoodpublishers.com

22 23 24 25 26 27 28 / 7 6 5 4 3 2 1

This book is dedicated to my "Sweet Girl," Lisa Fraze.
During the time in which this book was written, you . . .

battled breast cancer,

endured three major surgeries,

married off a son,

welcomed a new daughter to the family,

parented a teenage daughter,

buried a friend and mother-in-law,

completed your LPC,

worked a full-time job,

loved those in your life deeply,

have been the greatest wife to a
less than *greatest* husband,

and kept your focus on and faith
in Christ the entire time.

You are an incredible lady. I am a blessed man.

—**David**

I dedicate this book to my wife, Amy, who has been my spiritual partner, best friend, coparent, and cominister in youth ministry. Without you, my youth ministry would not be what it is today. I thank God for all the Bible studies, retreats, camps, and events that you have been at, serving teens by my side.

I also dedicate this to the primary recipients of my youth ministry, Madeline and Abby. You have been a source of agape love from the day you were born and I held you in my hands. Thank you for showing me Jesus in ways I could never have dreamed!

You three have been the best part of my youth ministry.

—**Walter**

CONTENTS

Acknowledgments 13

Foreword 15

Preface 19

Introduction 25

Affirmation Matters 31

Failure Matters 40

Conflict Matters 50

Friendship Matters 58

Serving Matters 64

Partnership Matters 75

Wisdom Matters 84

Discipleship Matters 93

Parenting Matters 102

Discipline Matters 109

Internships Matter 117

Hiring Matters 125

Firing Matters 136

Money Matters 147

Sabbath Matters 156

Conclusion: Where Do You Go from Here? 162

A Word on Sabbaticals 165

In Their Own Words 169

Sample Internship Agreement 183

Sample Job Offer Letter 185

Two Obvious Reminders 187

A Word on Disagreements 191

Hiring and Firing Resources 193

Notes 195

About the Authors 201

ACKNOWLEDGMENTS

Books like these do not happen in a vacuum; they come out of community. For me, this book comes from the different churches that have been so generous as to let me do youth ministry. Truth be told, I never planned on going into youth ministry; I kind of fell into it (a story for a different book). I owe my thirty years of youth ministry to God. Thanks to his work in my life, I have had the blessing to serve a variety of different teens, churches, elders, parents, and friends. I have had parents who have shown me tremendous amounts of unmerited grace, allowing me to keep on doing youth ministry by sharing their teens with me. I have had elders who loved me and allowed me to see Jesus in the wilderness seasons of ministry, when I had little to give. I have been fortunate to serve with a special group of youth ministers in California and Tennessee who have sharpened me to become better at following my calling. Most of all, I have been so richly blessed by the teens I have served over three decades, who have shown me Jesus, helped me learn Scripture, made me laugh uncontrollably, and helped my faith grow exponentially.

David, the hours we have spent dreaming, talking, laughing, eating, and now writing together have been a rich source of grace in my life. You are a brother, not biologically, but as close as one can be. I thank my God for all my remembrances of you.

—Walter

Writing a book takes a lot of work. While the authors' names appear on the front of the book, receiving the credit, unseen and unheralded are a host of individuals whose influence and inspiration are felt on each page. This is certainly the case for this book.

For over thirty years now, I have been, and continue to be, blessed by a host of passionate and talented parent and adult ministry partners. It is a dangerous game to name any of the myriad of names that come to my mind. A game I do not want to play. I will say, in the stories that accompany each chapter, many of these parent and adult friends will find themselves.

However, I will acknowledge two couples. Why? They not only continue to serve as faithful partners in ministry, but they were also participants in my son's wedding. Lisa and I have both lost our parents. When my son's wedding approached, Braeden asked these two families to be part of the ceremony. Kelley and Karen Rogers and Rick and Wendy Kemp filled in as my son's grandparents, and they represent the best of the ideals found in this book.

Walter Surdacki. Our adventures have been many. Our conversations, life changing. Our partnership in ministry, appreciated. You are a true friend and colleague.

—David

FOREWORD

What do youth pastors do when they're not youth pastoring?
Teenagers wonder this, often thinking youth leaders have the best
job ever—only working a few hours a few days a week. Senior
leaders wonder this, asking where the youth ministry budget went,
why the youth ministers are never in the office, or why they need
a vacation after a youth ministry trip (wasn't that a vacation?).
Parents wonder this too, often looking through the only lens that
really matters to them—the experiences of their own kids. A lot
of hope and focus is directed at youth leaders, and while they are
amazing, capable people, they also need your partnership.

One activity youth pastors do when they're not youth
pastoring is talk with other youth pastors—for ideas, support,
encouragement, and empathy. I've had the privilege of having
Walter and Dave as conversation partners over many years. I've
sat on the shores of Costa Mesa with Walter, working together
to serve youth leaders and students for regional events. I've
eaten dinner in his home and watched him make the weighty
decision of moving from pastor to professor. I've had conversations with Dave, frequently through the Fuller Youth Institute's numerous and varied research projects, and he has helped
support my Youth, Family, and Culture doctoral students. With

both, I've shared too many glorious cups of coffee with laughter, lament, self-reflection, and hopeful dreams. What I love about these guys is that they're still in it—still working hard for young people, using their experience, wisdom, education, and imaginations to animate the youth ministry conversation. They're the types of people you seek out because they won't try to sell you a gimmick, rest on their laurels, or stop growing themselves. When you're with them, you won't want to be like them, but you will want to become a better version of yourself.

Know that I'm being more than nostalgic. There often exists a rather odd relationship between youth leaders and invested adults. Everyone wants their teenagers to connect with Jesus, have a great youth group experience, and keep the faith beyond high school. But often, we adults rarely understand each other. Connection is usually limited to permission slips, monthly parent emails, the occasional exchange at church or the summer trip drop-off area, and awkward parent meetings. Most everyone wants more, but these connections are often too rushed, too short, too infrequent, and too vague.

Walter and Dave want to bring more clarity to the parent–youth leader partnership. So think of them as approachable, empathetic, reliable youth leaders who know how to build bridges. Listen to what they have to say because perhaps your youth leader is afraid or unsure of how to express these sentiments. Think of their advice as ways to take a step closer to your youth leaders. Some of Walter and Dave's suggestions will be more challenging than others, but you can bet that it's sound and flows from the fruit of their experiences—both failures and successes.

Let's be clear: Walter and Dave want to do more than achieve a forced partnership between parents and youth leaders. Instead, they're envisioning a harmonious one that will support your teenagers' faith journeys. Youth ministry is more than a formula, relevant tips and tricks, or an escape from the big, bad world. It has the potential to be an environment of faith, where life can be lived and processed together. Adults need to be on the same page about what youth ministry aims to be, or it'll create confusion for teenagers, frustration for families, and exhaustion for youth leaders. Walter and Dave point you to what matters most, relational trust, where adults believe the best in each other, support each other, extend grace toward one another, and bring out the best in one another. Young people, then, will not just know the gospel—they'll experience it. And together, everyone can be transformed.

Now we're talking.

This is a book you'll want to return to again and again. Make it your own:

Start with the chapters that are most important to you.

Dog-ear pages that move you.

Circle ideas you want to try.

Jot notes in the margins about what went well (and what didn't).

Cross out ideas that just won't work for you.

Write your own ideas, inspired by theirs.

Treat this book like a journal more than a coffee table book!

Also, remember this project holds the promise of creating new bridges while also revealing relational gaps. When we start paying attention to what it means for adults to work together, it may mean celebrating the best and healing the broken elements in our relationships:

Pain is real.

Perspectives may differ.

Success and failure populate every youth ministry.

Fears surface.

Disagreement is scary but can be a portal for growing together.

Trust takes time.

This book is loaded with practical advice but leads with one big question: Will you lean in? Being willing must be your starting point. Then let the journey begin.

May you . . .

. . . embrace the practical wisdom in this book.

. . . know that every step you take is a faithful one.

. . . remember that the support you give your youth leaders can help them stay healthier, grow as leaders, and invest longer in your community.

In other words, if you take Walter and Dave's words to heart, you could contribute to making youth ministry better for everyone. I, for one, am 100 percent behind that vision.

Grace and peace,

Rev. Dr. Steven Argue, PhD
associate professor of Youth, Family, and Culture at Fuller Theological Seminary; applied research strategist at Fuller Youth Institute; coauthor of *Sticky Faith Innovation: How Your Compassion, Creativity, and Courage Can Support Teenagers' Lasting Faith* and *Growing With: Every Parent's Guide to Helping Their Teenagers and Young Adults Thrive in Their Faith, Family, and Future*

PREFACE

There was a time we thought we could do anything as youth ministers. Reality shattered this idealistic notion rather quickly. To be clear, we believe youth ministry can do a great deal, have a tremendous positive impact, and be part of the fix, but it alone can't fix anything.

Youth ministry *can't* . . .

> . . . *fix your kid.* We can assist the church in providing a supportive environment in which students can ask and explore the answers to difficult questions, and we do have some good answers, but we are not professional therapists.

> . . . *fix your church.* We can assist the church in finding a vibrant missional direction forward. We have a lot to say about healthy practices and want to be part of the growth of the overall body of believers. However, a vibrant youth ministry does not guarantee that your broken church will be fixed. It will highlight the brokenness. Healthy ministries tend to shed light on the unhealthy parts of a church.

. . . fix your child's school life. We can assist the church in being a trusted, creative, and positive school resource, but we can't fix schools. We can provide great programs for public, private, and homeschool environments. However, youth ministry's biggest gift to our schools is helping disciple young women and men, their parents, and surrounding adults into people who bring a positive, Christlike, servant heart into their schools.

. . . make your kid popular. We can assist the church in creating an environment in which every student feels cherished, seen, and welcomed, but popularity is not on our agenda.

. . . fix you. We can assist you as you pursue Christ and his will for your life, but we can't fix you. Often, we have adult volunteers say that one of our events was just what they needed, and parents certainly benefit from serving and participating in youth ministry programming. But service and participation do not fulfill the need for personal growth and healing. Actually (and this may be painful to hear, though that is not our intention), *if you are using the youth ministry to "fix" yourself, you are not ready to serve and participate in youth ministry.*

You may be thinking, "What a downer." But we're just adjusting your expectations a bit. We acknowledge these failures and mistakes many adults make because we often find our students (both interns and new full-time ministers) involved in needless conflict with parents and church leaders who thought hiring a youth minister would "fix" all their problems and ensure smooth sailing.

THE USE OF THE TERMS *PARENT* AND *ADULT*

Words have meaning. We want you to know how we are using the words *parent* and *adult*. If it appears that we are using the words interchangeably at times, it's because we are. Why?

The use of these words is grounded in our understanding of psychosocial research and Deuteronomy 6:4–9:

> Hear, O Israel: The LORD our God, the LORD is one.
> Love the LORD your God with all your heart and
> with all your soul and with all your strength. These
> commandments that I give you today are to be on
> your hearts. Impress them on your children. Talk
> about them when you sit at home and when you
> walk along the road, when you lie down and when
> you get up. Tie them as symbols on your hands and
> bind them on your foreheads. Write them on the
> doorframes of your houses and on your gates.

These words are spoken to the community of believers (all adults). While parents would be included in this community, they are not specifically mentioned. Psychosocial research continues to demonstrate that the first influencer of a student's spiritual life, for good or ill, is their parents, but a close second influencer is the rest of the adult community surrounding that student.[1]

This research conclusion aligns perfectly with the Lord's directive to Israel. Parents and surrounding adults play a crucial role in the spiritual development of children (and adolescents). A sobering thought: your student and any other students you have contact with are following your spiritual lead! Perhaps that is why Jesus spoke so passionately and clearly about the importance of our influence in children's lives, as recorded in

Matthew 18:6, Mark 9:42, and Luke 17:2. (Stop a second, pick a Gospel, and read those verses.) The influences of both parents and other adults matter.

What about the role of youth ministers? We are definitely influencers, but lower on the list because we don't spend every day with the students. That's why, see above, the word *assist* is used repeatedly regarding the things a youth minister *can* do. In short, we *assist* parents and the surrounding adult community in the spiritual development of students.

So while we will differentiate between the terms *parent* and *adult* at times . . .

> . . . if you are a single adult volunteering in youth ministry, this book is for you.

> . . . if you are a married adult with no children volunteering in youth ministry, this book is for you.

> . . . if you are a married adult parent volunteering in youth ministry, this book is for you.

> . . . if you are a single adult parent volunteering in youth ministry, this book is for you.

> . . . if you are . . . you get the picture.

This book is for all those adults serving in or interested in the success of the ministry to youth in your church.

HOW TO READ THIS BOOK

All new appliances, computers, televisions, phones, power tools, gaming systems, and assembly-required furniture come with a full set of instructions for setup and use. However, because we are impatient and ready to use our purchase quickly, most of these come with a one-page, easy-to-understand set of quick start-up instructions.

I like the quick start instructions. Depending on the complexity of the device, most instruction guides are one to four pages max. The steps are easy to follow and filled with valuable information, and they typically let you know when you are out of your league and need to open up the complete set of instructions.

The book you are holding is a quick start guide for parents (adults) in youth ministry, and it's the second book in the Practical Wisdom series. Depending on the complexity of the topic, most chapters are concise. The steps are easy to follow and are sandwiched between actual youth ministry stories that highlight the need for and application of the truth being discussed. The information is arranged in three parts:

Why? Theological underpinnings and support for the truth

How? Practical application and discussion of the truth

Now? Suggestions for first steps in strengthening the truth or making the truth a part of your youth ministry context

Helpful endnotes are provided for clarification and deeper study. In short, there is no "right way" to read this book. You can read front to back or skip around to the topic you need quick start-up assistance with right now.

Wherever you start, thank you for allowing us to join you in your youth ministry journey.

INTRODUCTION

After many hours of labor and then an emergency C-section, I (Walter) officially became a father. I had been doing full-time youth ministry for about five years and had no idea what I was doing bringing a child into this world. Sure, I was great at leading a group of teens in a devotional on Romans 8 or organizing a New Year's Eve lock-in. But as soon as we got back to our apartment with our newborn daughter, I went to my bookshelf to find the manual. You know, the manual that tells you how to be a parent. How to "succeed" as a parent of an adolescent (I know, here I was with a week-old infant and already fast-forwarding to when my daughter would be in youth group). There weren't any of those kinds of books. Sure, there were those parenting books that told you what to expect when you're expecting. The ones that prepared you for lock-ins, weeks of camp, midweek Bible study, mission trips, and so on were missing . . . nonexistent.

That is why we wrote this book. This book helps you get ready for and then navigate those youth ministry years as a family. You heard that correctly: *as a family*. Youth group is not only for your teenager. Youth ministry, done well, includes and impacts the entire family. Your. Entire. Family.

This is not a book about how you have to make your teens sit down and have a family devotional. For those of you stressed about that, you can relax.

But this book will help you and your teen thrive and flourish during these important years. This book will give practical suggestions on how you can work alongside and support those leading your youth ministry.

We know this sounds imposing. Intimidating. Even frightening. We are here to guide you through the confusion, show you which pitfalls to avoid, and drop some wisdom that you can actually use.

Trust us, we have been there. You can do this.

THE CHANGING LANDSCAPE OF CONTEMPORARY YOUTH MINISTRY

"When I was your age . . ." We all heard that from our parents. And yes, we uttered that same phrase to our own teens. We are sure you have at least been tempted to use those words on your own children. However, there is a problem with this statement.

It is not true.

We were never their age.

Sure, there was a time in the past when we were chronologically their age. I was twelve years old sometime in the twentieth century (aka *last century*). However, my experience of being that age at that time in history, with its cultural ethos, was not like my children's twelve-year-old experience.

Things have changed dramatically. Technology is ubiquitous. Information is growing at exponential rates. The world has shrunk. Innocence is lost at a much earlier age. The issues and experiences our twelve-year-old teens are exposed to are tremendously different.

We did not have to worry about . . .

. . . online bullying twenty-four hours a day, seven days a week.

. . . how many likes a social media post got and how that reflects on someone's popularity.

. . . constructing a college application a mile long, filled with extracurriculars, honors courses, and volunteer hours, plus a 5.0 GPA.

. . . never having an off season—playing a sport twelve months a year just to be considered for a spot on the varsity squad.

. . . being tracked by Mom and Dad through our cell phone every moment of the day.

. . . increased rates of anxiety and depression.

. . . the easy availability of pornography on a smartphone.

. . . pressure to find and focus on a career before the age of eighteen.

YOUR YOUTH MINISTRY CANNOT BE THEIR YOUTH MINISTRY

Their world is different. That means, as parents, we are called to develop new tools and strategies to navigate these uncharted parenting waters. This also means their youth ministry world is going to be different. Sunday-night devotionals and an occasional lock-in may have sufficed for our spiritual development when we were in youth group. Today? The demands put upon a local youth minister to develop a comprehensive, theologically sound, biblically based program packed with the diversity to meet the needs of a wide variety of teens while making it "fun" (with a little N. T. Wright thrown in) is in a different league.

Youth ministry has changed. Never before in the history of youth ministry has there been as many books, websites, conferences, training opportunities, volunteers, and resources, or as much funding, as now. It began its infancy in local churches in the early 1970s, shifted to full-fledged adolescence in the 1990s, and is now emerging into adulthood. Sophisticated ministry philosophies, statistical research, and creative theology and praxis methodologies now occupy the youth ministry landscape. We are using these terms on purpose because these are the words and concepts we teach to our youth ministry students.

As a parent, it may be tempting to compare your personal experience with youth ministry to today's offerings and yearn for the "good ol' days." We need to realize that with these new challenges culture continues to throw our way, youth ministry programming is different. Actually, youth ministers have been doing a great job of adapting and transforming, often on the fly, to meet the rising challenges of contemporary youth ministry practice. Yes, the "good ol' days" are gone, but one key element remains the same.

A MOMENT OF HONEST TRUTH

One of the dirty little secrets we need to let you in on is this: There has never been a time in church history when there has been such a high level of dedicated resources, as stated above, given to youth ministry. There has also never been a time in church history that we have seen so many teens and emerging adults leaving the church. Bottom line: What we have been doing has not been working. The research out there definitely shows that the best way to disciple and raise students in faith is to surround and immerse them with believing parents and other adults.[1] The National Study of Youth and Religion, the gold standard for adolescent spirituality research, has shown that the adolescents and young adults who continue in the faith are those who had parents and other adults integrated into and throughout their faith practices.[2]

Parents and adults remain the link to the "good ol' days." Yes, programming looks different (sorry, the lock-in is not making a comeback anytime soon), but the impact parents and adults have in a student's spiritual formation is vital. To put it bluntly, if your student doesn't "get" faith, the first place to look is in your own home and surrounding adult community. As Fraze says, "We can't out-teach what happens in your home or surrounding adult community. We are not that good."

Now that we may have struck the fear of God into you, we do want to assure you that while things are radically different, things have also remained the same. We can take courage in the fact that "Jesus Christ is the same yesterday and today and forever" (Heb. 13:8). No change in culture can change who God is and what he wants for us. There are constants that God has graciously given us that parents can rest upon.

AFFIRMATION MATTERS

Everybody Needs to Hear "Good Job" Once in a While.
The Youth Minister Is Part of Everybody.

The year 2020 was a challenging one for everybody.

The global pandemic and resulting shutdowns, racial and political divisions, job and financial concerns, and all the personal struggles embedded in each of these were, and continue to be, challenges.

2020 changed the way we "did" church and youth ministry programming:

The retreat weekend? Canceled.

The summer camp? Canceled.

The weekly gathering? Canceled.

The mission trip? Canceled.

In short, a lot of the typical youth ministry activity that determined and defined healthy ministry programming was canceled.

A discussion for another time: The canceling of the "typical" gave churches and youth ministries a unique opportunity, one ministries were in need of, to reflect on and evaluate what ministry activities are really needed, or are working, to reach the world and followers of Christ.

While necessary, such times are difficult because the markers we use to measure our "success" are taken away:

> How was the retreat weekend? I don't know; it was canceled.

> How was summer camp this year? I don't know; it was canceled.

> How is the weekly gathering going? I don't know; we haven't met in months.

> How did the mission trip go? I don't know; it was canceled.

Yes, youth ministers creatively adapted and are continuing to adapt programming, but the markers of whether these adaptations will produce a healthy ministry are yet to be determined. The result? Discouragement. Pressure. Doubt.

Discouragement in knowing what we used to do can't work or isn't working.

Pressure from parents and students who can't shake "the way things used to be" syndrome and complain about change.

Doubt as to whether we are equipped to adapt programming and whether the "new" programming will be embraced and supported or lead to our removal.

Think about it! Because of cancelations, 2020 marked the first year I (David) had not spent at least a week at summer camp since *I* was in sixth grade!

For me, the answers to my personal discouragement, pressure, and doubt came from a simple note through Facebook Messenger. A mother thanked me for the time I spent with her son at a recent lunch. That was enough.

TRUTH: AFFIRMATION MATTERS

WHY?

This is a negative way to start this section, but it is purposeful. Affirmation is needed because some people are not well-suited for official, paid involvement in youth ministry. Did I really say that? Yes. Let me be clear and explain (I am probably not talking about what some of you are imagining).

We, parents and church leaders, at times have given our affirmation to youth pastors because they are cool, young, athletic, artistic, or attractive, or because they have a popular presentation style. Sure, these factors are impactful, but there is so much more to a minister's work with students and the church than his or her ability to "relate" to young people.

As they relate, can they communicate Scripture in-depth? That is, can they help students wrestle with difficult life situations and questions? Or do they just identify and relate to the struggle?

As they relate, can they connect with other adults? In other words, do they surround themselves with volunteers who are also cool, young, athletic, artistic, attractive people with popular presentation styles? Or do they make room for the other, less talented adults in their ministry program?

As they relate, do they show favoritism toward those who look like your kid and/or the type of families you want hanging out with your kid? Or do they relate with a wide variety of students/families?

As they relate, do they focus more on programming quality and execution than relationship building? Yes, programming quality and execution are important. Youth ministers need to be able to conceive of, organize, budget for, and execute programs. However, does your youth minister want to build or have the ability to build relationships with more than just the teenagers in your church? If not, why?

I realize I am on the edge of an argument with this line of questioning. Again, it is imperative that we examine why we affirm a person's calling to work with us in discipling our most precious resource, students. Yes, relatability is important, but so is depth of biblical knowledge, adolescent development, family dynamics, and cultural understanding.

When a decision is made to work with a youth minister, affirmation of that choice is important. Consider these key affirmations into ministry:

Moses's affirmation of Joshua. In Deuteronomy 32:44, Moses brought Joshua with him when he spoke his last words to the people of Israel. This was a visual representation of affirmation, signaling that Joshua would replace Moses as leader of the young nation of Israel. When looking at his life and experiences, Joshua is a clear choice for leadership.

The Jerusalem council's affirmation of Barnabas and Paul. In Acts 15, the council of church leaders in Jerusalem affirmed the ministry of Barnabas and Paul before the new gentile believers through a letter. They further affirmed their mission by sending Judas (not that one) and Silas to help with the ministry. When looking at the unique experiences of both Barnabas and Paul with the gentile world, they were the clear choice for leadership.

Paul's affirmation of Timothy. In the letter of 2 Timothy, Paul affirms, encourages, and challenges the ministry of his intern (as we would call him now) Timothy. Paul gives him a short history lesson and reminds him of what he has seen and experienced. Paul's farewell affirmation, during which he tells Timothy to follow his lead, is particularly meaningful. When looking at his life and experience, Timothy's choice for leadership is clear.

Other biblical examples show God's affirmation of ministry (Isaiah 6 provides a really good example), but the ones above are provided to show how God's people affirm each other for ministry. As we read these various accounts in Scripture, we see letters, prayers, witnesses, laying on of hands, and words of encouragement being used to embolden the recipients to fulfill the challenging work of ministry.

Not only is affirmation important in the call to a certain ministry, but it provides a level of encouragement to continue on in the most trying of circumstances:

* God gave Abraham affirmation that his ministry would be rewarded (Gen. 15).
* God gave Moses affirmation that his ministry would end with Israel arriving to and living in the promised land (Deut. 32).
* Paul gave Timothy affirmation that the sacrifice of ministry was worth the reward (2 Tim. 3).

Affirmation of the call to ministry and a ministry's effectiveness provides valuable encouragement and acknowledges that a minister's personal and professional attributes are wanted and needed. The removal of that affirmation lets the minister know that his or her time with a certain church is over. In some cases, as alluded to earlier, this helps the individual realize his or her call to paid ministry *was a mistake.*

HOW?

Here are ways to give meaningful affirmation during three key times in a youth minister's journey with your church.

At the Beginning

Starting a ministry in a positive, meaningful way is important. First moments provide memories for both the minister and church that are helpful to fall back on when times are tough and resolve is fading. Preferably in the main assembly, but certainly in a special assembly of parents and students, affirmation should be given in the midst of a public gathering:

Affirmation of the Call

The formality of words and ordination procedures will vary by denomination. However, the church family should hear from senior leadership (preferably a senior pastor) that the youth minister being asked to join the church is both qualified and called to his or her position of service.

Affirmation of Support

Again, the formality of words and ordination procedures will vary by denomination, but the church family should hear from senior leadership (preferably a senior pastor) that the youth minister has the leadership's professional and personal support. Furthermore, it is my opinion that each church member should be asked to give an affirming yes to assisting the new minister in the work of discipling the youth.[1]

Both of these affirmations should be followed with a time of prayer. The laying on of hands by congregational leaders as part of this prayer time is a special, affirming action for both the minister and his or her family.

During Their Ministry

As mentioned above, ongoing affirmation for ministry and ministry effectiveness provides valuable encouragement and support to your youth minister. Here are several ways to show your affirmation:

> *Written statements.* Letters, notes, or electronic communications of affirmation are appreciated by youth ministers. These encouraging statements are kept in files and treasured. These should be purely encouragement, not encouragement layered on top of a complaint.

> *Time off.* Unless it is an emergency, protect and honor your youth minister's family time, days off, and vacation time. If you are close enough, gently remind your youth ministers that you expect them to have lives outside of the student ministry and to take time for themselves.

> *Time with.* Affirmation is given when you serve with someone in the ministry. Make certain that your youth minister never has to "beg" for volunteers. Join in the ministry willingly and enthusiastically, and encourage other adults to do the same.

> *Gifts.* Youth ministers do not do what they do for gifts. With that said, surprising them with movie tickets or

a DoorDash meal or offering to let them stay at your vacation property for a day off or weekend is special and demonstrates affirmation of the time and effort they are spending with your students.

Words. This is a low-cost, high-impact affirmation. Look your youth ministers in the face and thank them for their work and presence in your life. Be sure to thank their spouses and families as well.

At the end. Yes, if the separation with your youth minister is a negative one, it will impact how the ending is celebrated. If possible, celebrate all that the Lord has accomplished while the youth ministers worked with your ministry, repeating all the steps involved with the beginning of their time with your church. *Affirm* the youth minister's call, and *support* the ministry they are joining.

Special affirmation idea. One of the most special affirmation ideas for acknowledging and celebrating your minister leaving for another youth ministry happens when senior leaders from both locations agree to join the other church family for the beginning and ending affirmation ceremonies. Past leadership can give a parting blessing while new leadership offers a blessing of acceptance and thanksgiving. This takes a high level of cooperation, especially if you feel the other church is "stealing" your youth minister, but provides a great deal of closure for that minister.

NOW?

Get to affirming your youth ministers. May I suggest you put this book down for a moment and write a quick note of affirmation to them. (You can choose the method of delivery, but don't mention the book that made you do it!)

Again, 2020 was a challenge for everyone, not just youth ministers.

❉

I (David) remember one moment when such an affirmation made all the difference. I had just completed one of the most difficult weeks of ministry in my life (and I have had a few). Instead of a weekend of rest, I was off to a speaking engagement.

I was tired.

I was a bit discouraged.

I wondered what, if anything, I had to give the audience before me.

As I opened my Bible to preach, unaware, I found a note placed by a friend:

> *Don't worry about the perceptions of others—real or imagined.*
>   *Don't waste time comparing yourself to others.*
>   *Be Real. Be You.*
>
>   *Love you, Bro.*

A much-needed reminder.

TRUTH: AFFIRMATION MATTERS

FAILURE
MATTERS

Your Youth Minister Is Going to Fail.
What Are You Going to Do about It?

"We will have two travel days!" I (David) said confidently.

This short mission trip to Daytona Beach, Florida, began and ended on a note of failure. From my view as a twenty-four-year-old youth minister, the roughly 1,429-mile journey from Lubbock, Texas, to Daytona Beach, Florida, was not only feasible but preferable to a shorter one.

On paper, the actual mission experience was going to be incredible, but the failure in travel planning created tired and cranky participants. The twenty-plus-hour trip actually ended up taking twenty-five hours because I did not factor in stops for meals, gas, and the restroom. It was an emotional, tiring two days of hard travel that ended up impacting the quality of work we did with our partnering church.

Fail.

I got a lot of "feedback" on how bad my trip planning was, but I was given the opportunity to grow and learn from the experience. An experience for which, twenty-seven years later, the alumni of that trip still make fun of me.

Needless to say, my trip planning improved drastically the next summer.

TRUTH: FAILURE MATTERS

 WHY?

The Bible is filled with failure. Read that last sentence again; I will wait. Failure is not to be "celebrated" or "accepted" without challenge (Rom. 6), but it is to be expected as a normal part of personal, spiritual, and professional growth. Failure is faced by our most beloved and elevated heroes of the Bible:

Adam and Eve	Well, you know about their choice in trees.
Abraham	He had some trouble relying on his own armed force, lying, and reproducing.
Sarah	She laughed and gave her servant to her husband.
Joseph	He may have been a bit too proud of his dream-interpreting abilities.
Moses	He murdered an Egyptian guard. Oh, and the whole placing-himself-in-the-position-of-God thing with the water-out-of-the-rock episode?
Samson	He gave up his gift of strength because he had a habit of not saying no to beautiful women.
Lot's wife	A reminder to not get salty.
David	Where do we start? Adultery, murder, dishonesty, pride, revenge, and more are on his list of failures.
Peter	Well, he cut a guy's ear off and denied Jesus. And . . . he struggled with racism.
Paul	He took Christians into custody and presided over the execution of Stephen.

41

You may have been uncomfortable and had to fact-check some of those. Why? For most of us, we concentrate on the highlight reels of biblical heroes (Heb. 11) and downplay or ignore the blooper reels that make them the great examples of faith they truly are. Fact: for every failure listed above, you can see how God used these moments to refine, discipline, and grow each of these giants of faith. In short, *failure is not fatal*. However, read carefully, because failures do have teachable moments—consequences:

Adam and Eve	They had to live outside the Garden.
Abraham	He had trouble with Lot and Ishmael.
Sarah	She developed and fought a bad case of jealousy.
Joseph	He ended up in a pit.
Moses	He spent forty years in the desert.
Lot's wife	She became a pillar of salt.
Samson	He lost his eyesight and then his life.
David	He lost his son(s) and his kingdom (though he found it again) and brought death on Israel.
Peter	He was in a dark place for a while.
Paul	He was feared and misunderstood.

As you can see, not all consequences are the same, because not all failures are the same. However, there are consequences. Here is the great news, though: God does not waste the pain of failure. Take some time to read Hebrews 12:4–12. Yes, the topic of conversation is the discipline of hardships, but the actions of God, as seen in the lives of the heroes above, are normative. If we allow him to (another topic for another time), God will use our failure as an opportunity to help us grow and learn.

HOW?

Failure happens. You can't cut Romans 3:23, "For all have sinned," out of your Bible. In the original Greek, *all* means . . . well, "all." *You will* make that awkward call to the youth minister to inform her that your kid did something wrong and ask for her help. *You will* hear words coming out of your mouth and/or witness your actions and feel like a failure as a parent. *You will* be disappointed in your church leaders (even your favorite go-to [in order to complain] leader). Your youth minister will fail (more than once) and *you will* be angered by his lack of judgment and ability. How do we handle such failure as youth group parents?

A Little Word about Failure

Admittedly, the term *failure* is a rather subjective word in the context of youth ministry. Are we talking about moral failure? Maybe. Are we talking about a failure in judgment? Sure. Are we talking about a failure in planning? Perhaps. Is the youth minister failing to "do" ministry in the way you experienced it as a kid? We certainly hope so. A youth minister may fail in these and more areas. Regardless, the suggestions below will be helpful. It is up to you to manage your definitions.

Manage Your Emotions

Parents can get *really* fired up when they perceive that someone else's failure has impacted the life of their kid. We are parents; we know and can identify with that kind of frustration and anger. Slowing your emotional reaction is the first step in working through the scenario you are facing. Yes, the size of the failure impacts the strength of your reaction and your ability to give someone a break. Still, even though it's difficult, stepping away and cooling off before engaging your youth minister is extremely helpful. The last thing you want as a parent is to create an us-versus-them scenario. As parents, we confess that in our flesh, that scenario is what we want to lead with. However, managing our emotions enables us to get a clearer picture of the situation and place the failure at the feet of those truly responsible. *On more than one occasion*, parents have ended up apologizing for their initial explosion of emotion because, in the process of discovery, they realized it was their own child's failure that caused the problem.

Consequences, Grace, and Forgiveness

Failures have consequences. Without consequences, there is no growth or learning. This is not a parenting book, but a book on how to help your youth minister be successful. Still, we bet some of you have made statements similar to these to your student:

"I will lock you in that room for the remainder of high school because you . . ."

"I will have the keys to your car for a year if you . . ."

"I will ground you until graduation if I have to . . ."

"I brought you into the world and . . ."

As parents, we often say things that are beyond reason (and we have a great time doing it). But if, as parents of children in youth ministry, you respond to the failure of your youth minister that way, it could lead to their being fired. That may be the logical consequence of their action(s). But be careful what you speak into the air:

"If I was the preacher at this church, I would fire that youth minister and . . ."

"She needs to be fired for the way she hurt my kid's feelings . . ."

"He is reckless and needs to be fired for the way he drives that van . . ."

"What were we thinking when we hired this minister?"

Failure should not be ignored, but the consequences should be measured and fitting to produce growth and learning. For example, if your youth minister is an unsafe driver, confront her lovingly and let her know what you have witnessed and your concerns. Believe it or not, that usually works. However, if you approach her in a belittling and threatening manner, don't be surprised if she is defensive in response. As in most situations, failure can be addressed frankly with a positive outcome when approached correctly.

What if she doesn't listen and continues to drive recklessly? No problem. Follow Jesus's principles of conflict in Matthew 18:15–20. Take someone with you to witness the conversation. As always, your approach should be loving and kind.

Simply put, instead of calling for the removal of the youth minister in the midst of failure, *manage your emotions*, share your wisdom, and process the situation until you've truly located who is responsible. In other words, you may be wrong in placing the blame for the failure on the youth minister. *Hard truth time*: more often than we would like to admit, a youth minister is held responsible and terminated for a failure he is not responsible for—one that should be placed at the feet of the church leaders who hired him.

With all failure, grace and forgiveness are essential. Even when consequences lead to the youth minister's dismissal, grace and forgiveness should permeate the process of departure. With that said, remember, *failures have consequences*. Protecting youth ministers from the consequences of their failures, in the name of grace and forgiveness, is not what we are suggesting; such action denies the youth ministers opportunities for growth and learning. What we do suggest is an emotionally managed, logical, consequential approach to failure.[1]

Working through the Failure

Scott Cormode, leadership guru and conflict specialist from Fuller Seminary, says the following should be spoken out loud at the beginning of a difficult conversation: "This situation will not undo us."[2] What a wonderful statement that has been designed to differentiate the issue (failure at hand) from the person (who they are). Again, the mindset we have when we begin working through a failure is crucial.

This simple Five-P Process will help you work through failure with your youth minister:

Private. If not a matter of life and death, have the discussion about the youth minister's failure in private and in person. If meeting in person is not an option, call. Avoid the temptation to send an angry text or email.

Personal. Speak about what concerns *you* and your student. Furthermore, avoid venting your feelings to other parents or church leaders. This does nothing more than fan the flames of failure. As mentioned, if you do not feel heard, take a witness with you, but don't start your conversation with ambiguous and threatening statements like "Many of my friends . . ." Speak only about those things that affect you and your teen.

If others are affected, let them address it themselves. Yes, there are failures that need direction from others in leadership. However, if you are the type of parent who skips the youth minister and goes straight to the senior pastor or church leadership team with your concerns, stop it. Such actions are the mark of a coward, and they are destructive. (Jesus had a lot to say about this in Matthew 18.)

Pursue. Pursue a path forward that provides growth and learning for the youth minister and yourself. In other words, go into the meeting with the goal of being heard and listening to the youth minister. Again, emotions will run hot, but keep in the front of your mind the conviction that "this situation will not undo us" when working through and pursuing a positive outcome to the failure. Pursue forgiveness as well. Even though it is difficult, modeling this behavior for young people has a deep and lasting impact on their spiritual and societal development.

Progress. Accountability is important in working through failure. Following the same process above, check back in with the youth minister about the progress everyone is making in regard to the issue you discussed.

Praise. When the failure has been resolved and/or learned from, acknowledge the correction and thank your youth minister. This type of praise deepens your relationship and shows that you are truly partners in ministry. Praise also indicates that you are pursuing forgiveness and the relationship is appropriately being restored.

NOW?

You will not have to wait long before you face a failure (real or perceived) in the youth ministry. Some will be simple ones: miscommunication, tardiness, an unpleasant moment for your student, lost luggage from a trip. Though not as common, there will also be more serious failures: programming that does not meet agreed-upon expectations, for instance, or moral failure on the part of the youth minister or your student.

Whatever the situation, whether you are working through a failure at this moment or not, be prepared:

Decide. Before a failure occurs, decide now that it will be handled appropriately and with the grounding mindset that "this will not undo us."

Commit and practice. If not now, at some point, your youth minister will fail. Commit to and practice the above suggestions.

Pray. This is the beginning and ending point of working through all failures. If you want to handle these times with grace and forgiveness, God has to be invited into and remain in the middle of every tense, frustrating, and difficult conversation.

"So you were just being mean?" asked the student.

"Yes," I (David) said with sadness and embarrassment. I had no other answer to give; I had failed.

One summer at camp, I had a young staff member who was really scared of bears. I mean *really* afraid. As a joke, my intern and I created fake bear tracks and scratch marks outside his cabin one night. When he woke up for his camp staff duties, we pointed out the tracks and scratches. He was freaked out, and we laughed. That was day one.

We continued our joke for three days. Needless to say, he lost sleep and was on edge. Harmless, right? Not when the real bears (yes, I said *bears*, plural) started combing through camp. We called the staff together and instructed them to be sure they cleaned the areas they were responsible for well and to remove any food items they may have stored in their cabins. This young man freaked out! An all-out, snot-producing-tears kind of freak-out.

As I comforted and reassured this young man, I recognized that it was confession time. That is when he asked if I had just been being mean, and I gave him my honest answer. Fail. The look of disappointment in his eyes and the pain in my heart—I will never forget that moment.

Needless to say, my days of making myself and others laugh at a student's expense ended. That failure allowed me to see life from another's perspective.

TRUTH: FAILURE MATTERS

CONFLICT
MATTERS

It Is Not a Matter of If, but When!
Conflict Will Happen, So Be Ready.

"It is obvious you have been listening to John! All of the hard work we did, and have been doing before you got here, was for nothing!" This was the angry response I (David) got from a key volunteer after one of my first leadership meetings.

Emotions were heightened. Passionate sides taken. We both had a choice: work through the conflict in a productive fashion, or let it destroy and splinter our relationship and ministry together.

We chose to be productive. The results? Tremendous!

We examined the issue from both sides and chose a third, mutually accepted step forward for the youth ministry. The conflict served as a catalyst for change and provided a clear path forward.

What would have happened if the conflict destroyed our relationship and ministry together? Youth ministry programming would have suffered. And personally, I would have missed out on one of the richest, most authentic, and most treasured ministry partnerships and friendships I have ever known and continue to enjoy.

For the record, this was merely the first of our "disagreements." There have been several since, and I am sure there are more to come. I am counting on it.

TRUTH: CONFLICT MATTERS

WHY?

Conflict happens. It is difficult to read the Bible without coming across some sort of conflict narrative. However, today, those of us in "church life" often go out of our way to avoid conflict (another discussion for another time), and we miss out on dynamic, "iron sharpening" (Prov. 27:17) growth moments when we do. To be clear, I am not talking about being an argumentative, selfish, divisive, church member (or church leader).[1] There is plenty of Scripture speaking against such behavior.[2] I am talking instead about entering conflict situations with the goal of reaching mutual understanding (I did not say agreement) and determining a mutually beneficial path forward for both conflicted parties.

Consider the positive outcomes of these two famous conflict narratives. Both are found in Acts 15 and involve the same two rather well-known players:

The Jerusalem council. When gentiles came to faith in Jesus Christ, the racial tension between them and Jewish believers needed to be addressed quickly before it threatened the unity of the early church. This council addressed the issue practically through "much discussion," appeals to Scripture, personal testimonies from both parties, consultation with other believers, and prayer. What resulted was a clear articulation of the problem (mutual understanding) and a practical solution for both Jew and gentile believers (mutually beneficial path forward).

Paul and Barnabas. These two close friends had a "sharp" disagreement over whether Mark should be allowed to join them on their missionary journey. Because Mark had "deserted" the two during a previous journey, Paul did not want the young man to join them. Barnabas wanted to bring Mark and give the young man another opportunity. This conflict was settled by Paul and Barnabas agreeing to disagree (mutual understanding) and going their separate ways on the mission journey (mutually beneficial path forward). It must be understood that they still did not agree. But they also did not destroy the person or ministry of the other.

Both of these stories demonstrate how church life, like all of life, is indeed a conflict-rich environment. The beauty of these two narratives is found in the way each ended with mutual understanding and a mutually beneficial path forward.

Inevitably, your youth ministry is in one of three phases: it is currently going through a conflict, just journeyed through a conflict, or is about to have a conflict. We do not mean to be fatalistic, just realistic.

Conflict should not be needlessly stirred up or sought out, but conflict happens.

HOW?

As you can see, the question is not *if* but *when* conflict will happen. Actually, this may sound strange, but like in any relationship, I hope there is a bit of conflict between you and your youth minister because it's an indicator that both parent and youth minister are partnering in the process of discipling students. It also indicates that both parties care deeply about the ministry. Here are a few suggestions for working through conflict with your youth minister and arriving at a mutually beneficial conclusion. Yes, I came up with an acrostic to help commit these steps to memory:

> *Commit.* Decide now that this conflict will end in an appropriate relationship with your youth minister or church family. This statement needs some unpacking. What is meant by *appropriate relationship*? The conflict may conclude with a negotiated, adjusted relationship. For instance, you may need to take a break from volunteering, your student may need to take a break from participating in a trip, you may decide not to be around the minister or ministry, or, in extreme cases, the youth minister may have to step away from his or her job. Regardless, decide in advance to treat each other as children of God.

> *Articulate.* Do not speak around the particulars of your conflict; be clear with your concerns. With that said, be aware of your tone and the way your words could be perceived. This can be *extremely* difficult, especially when the conflict involves your own student (as it often does). Regardless, do your part to stay as calm as possible. Please know that more than likely, your youth minister has been trained to listen and calmly respond as well.

Again, from personal experience, when it is your kid involved, emotions are often raw and volatile; do your best. Also, do not talk about your conflict with others. Jesus instructs us in Matthew 18 to deal directly with the person we have an issue with.

Listen. There are always (at least) two sides to a conflict. The other side may have a weak position, but there is still another side. Listen. More than once, after a parent had articulated his or her conflictual concern(s), I have responded with a very different side of the story. Often, mutual understanding and a mutually beneficial path forward quickly followed. Listen.

Look. Look toward the future as you work with your youth minister to identify a mutually beneficial path forward out of conflict. This involves being reasonable with your "demands." I hate to use that word, but this is often how the conversations that move us forward begin. For instance, if your student has missed all the mandatory training meetings for the upcoming mission trip to Brazil, should you really "demand" that they be able to participate? Look to the future and ask yourself what will happen to your student's spiritual growth, your reputation as a parent, and the reputation of the youth minister if your "demand" is granted. Perhaps your student needs to experience the consequences of his or her own actions.

By now, you have figured out the acrostic, CALL. Why? A lot of your conflicts, while best discussed face-to-face, will start with a phone call. *Commit. Articulate. Listen. Look.*

This should be a given, because the following are discussed in greater detail in this book, but remember these Bible-based principles on handling conflict:

Go directly to your youth minister with your conflict. Frankly, even though we know better, it is easy and "feels good" to air your grievances to other parents. You may need a bit of wise counsel from someone, but get the conversation going with your youth minister ASAP.

Speak for yourself and not "others." In short, if the "others" want to remain anonymous, then they are not ready to join the process of mutual understanding and finding a mutually beneficial path forward. If you use the word "others," don't be surprised if your youth minister asks you to identify these "others." Such talk is a power play and will prove unproductive.

Pray. Prayer should bathe the entire conflict process. Prayer invites the Lord into the conflict as a witness to both our attempt at mutual understanding and our agreement on a mutually beneficial path forward.

Show humility. Your conflict may be misplaced and/or caused by a misunderstanding. Students may lie in order to cover up their own messes. Be humble as you listen to the other side. And if your student is not lying, be humble with your rebuke. There is no need for a victory lap (no matter how much you want to take one).

Bring in church leadership when needed. Follow the directions of Jesus in Matthew 18. Go to your minister on your own with your concern, go back again with a witness, and then go to your church leadership (those who oversee the youth minister). CALL should be practiced with all three.

NOW?

First, *get ready*. Again, remember that it is not a matter of *if* but *when* conflict will occur. Go ahead and memorize the CALL steps.

Then, *get going*. When you are in the midst of a conflict with your youth minister, practice the CALL steps.

Finally, *get right*. If you are an argumentative, selfish, divisive church member (or church leader), repent and commit to being part of a solution instead of a problem. Oh, and if you think you are not one of those who needs to "get right," ask your spouse or trusted friend if they agree with your assessment.

❁

"Samuel is not coming to the youth group because of the way you are treating his friend Mike!"

The parent was clearly upset and disturbed by the reason Samuel gave them as to why he did not want to attend the youth group.

I called a meeting with Samuel, Mike, and their families. I invited my lead ministry volunteer, Tom, to witness.

After prayer, I said, "Mike, Samuel is telling his parents that he is not coming to the youth group because of the way I am treating you. I hate that you feel this way. I have invited Tom to listen to your response and hold me accountable to whatever I have done to hurt you and Samuel's participation with our ministry. Can you explain your feelings?" Then I waited.

What followed the awkward pause was the "other side" of the conflict. The result was mutual understanding and a mutually beneficial path forward. Both came back to the youth group and the parents of each student realized Mike's problem with me was my holding him and his friends accountable for how they were treating others in the youth ministry—a young man had actually left our ministry and his school because of their bullying.

Oh, I am still in touch with both Samuel and Mike. They are wonderful young men.

The conflict made us better.

TRUTH: CONFLICT MATTERS

FRIENDSHIP
MATTERS

Getting to Know Your Youth Minister as an Adult Is One of the Best Ways to Support Your Youth Minister.

"All my friends are teens."

That was spoken by a friend of mine in youth ministry after he had been doing youth ministry for about six years. Don't get me wrong, he loved the teens in his youth group. What he recognized though was he didn't have much interpersonal interaction with other adults. You know, grown-up time. Many of his conversations with teens centered around the latest music trends, video game themes, and Netflix binges. He was realizing he missed nuanced discussions on faith, politics, and finances.

You know, adulting.

His problem was likely exacerbated by the church around him. When he was seen spending time with teens from the youth group, attending games and plays at the local high school, and interacting with them at other events, the church happily believed that he was just doing his job. It was easy for adults in the church to assume that at other times, he was maintaining healthy boundaries in his personal life by spending time with other adults.

Without regular interaction and friendship with other adults, a youth minister can become isolated and extremely lonely. Why? Not only do they miss out on conversations and relationships one can only have with other adults, but teens grow up, graduate, and move out to attend college. If a youth minister's friend group is only the youth group, a youth minister loses a significant percentage of their friends to college every year.

TRUTH: FRIENDSHIP MATTERS

WHY?

This is one of those areas that Jesus modeled wonderfully. All throughout his ministry, we see Jesus spending time with all kinds of people from a variety of backgrounds:

* He hangs out with his friends at a wedding at Cana, where he winds up making wine (adulting).
* He goes on a men's retreat with Peter, James, and John to the Mount of Transfiguration.
* He engages in political debate with tax collectors.
* He has deep theological discussions with scribes and Pharisees.
* He spends a lot of time eating meals with others.

Much of a youth minister's task is that of a cultural anthropologist. In order to know how to contextualize the Bible for an adolescent audience, the youth minister must be immersed in adolescent culture. The danger is that one runs the risk of losing contact with the wider adult world and perspective. Jesus's example helps put into perspective the need for a youth pastor to practice establishing healthy boundaries.

HOW?

There are a number of ways that parents came into my own and my family's lives and built friendships that have lasted to this day. These are many of our most valued relationships. Here are a few ideas of how to do the same for your youth minister.

Grab Lunch Together

This isn't rocket science. Invite your youth minister to lunch. Obviously, if this is a one-on-one lunch, best practice dictates that these should be with someone of the same gender in order to remain above reproach. However, some of our favorite memories are times when my whole family was invited out to lunch after church or over to a youth group family's home for dinner. Getting to know each other in a casual setting apart from the church building is tremendously life-giving. Conversations about how we met our spouses, what we studied in college, places we have traveled, and the like really help us better understand and care for one another.[1]

Recreate Together

I believe there is something tremendously theological about recreation time. It is no wonder that the root of the word *recreation* is "re-creation." When we play, we are re-created through our leisure time. I befriended two or three youth group dads who loved to ski, and we lived three hours away from some excellent slopes in Lake Tahoe. We would generally get away to ski for the day a few times each season. While skiing was the excuse for us to spend time together, its importance was secondary. I always looked forward to the hours spent driving with other men that I respected and admired. We still, to this day, text one another whenever we have just had a great day on a mountain.

Show Hospitality

We were blessed to have been invited on a few occasions to vacation with some families from our youth group. What was notable about these times was the fact that we were not asked to be a youth minister for their teens on vacation; we vacationed with them. It was truly a way of doing life together and not a work event. Again, the hours spent together were foundational to building lasting friendships. While there were times they asked for parenting advice from me and my wife, two "cultural anthropologists," it also gave us time to learn about parenting from those who came before us.

Celebrate a Day of Sabbath/Accountability

A colleague in youth ministry once mentioned a very wise practice she had picked up. She said, "I intentionally don't spend time with teens on my day off so that when I have a fiancé or spouse, I won't have to carve out that time." Wow! What wisdom! She went on to say that some of those days off were filled with playing video games or doing laundry, but she wanted to make sure her boundaries were sufficiently built up for times she knew she would need them. The second thing this did was help create a margin for adult time. She said, "When someone from church or a friend of mine asked to spend time with me socially, I knew I could count on Thursdays; I already had that carved out of my schedule to be available."

One of the great things you can do as a good friend of your youth ministers is to ask them about their Sabbath or day off.

Help them remember to take this dedicated time of rest. And if appropriate, ask them out to lunch on that day every once in a while. The other thing you can do is be an outspoken advocate for protecting those boundaries when others, even elders or leadership, try to infringe on them.

NOW?

OK, you want to check that your youth minister has adult friends. Or, better yet, you want to deepen your friendship with your youth minister. So what do you do now?

First, *stop making assumptions.* It is so easy to assume someone else is checking in on your youth minister's health. Stop it. Do something. Give them a call, send a text, or make it a point to visit with them at the next youth gathering.

Then, *have the hard conversation.* It probably is not going to be a hard conversation for your youth minister, but it may be for you. Why? Because you do not want to appear as a meddling, overly concerned youth ministry parent. But trust me, your youth minister will appreciate this kind of concern. Here are a couple of conversation prompts:

> "Hey Jill, how is your day off going? I appreciate all you do for my son, but want to be sure you are taking time for yourself."

> "Hey Jill, I don't want to be intrusive, but I appreciate your relationship and the time you spend with my daughter and want to be sure you spend time with your friends as well. Do you have people, other than our students, who you get to spend time with outside of work?"

Trust me, the rest of the conversation will take care of itself. Have that hard conversation.

"We are going to teach the youth ministry class for the next month!"

These were the words my youth leaders approached my wife and me (David) with after a Sunday morning worship assembly. At first, I was offended by the demand and thought of their offer as a slap in the face, an implication that I wasn't capable of doing my job. Thankfully, they continued, "We just realized, you have been teaching every youth class for the last few years, and we think you need to spend some time with people your own age, develop some 'nonteen' relationships, and get some rest."

Once I better understood their motivation, their initiative was appreciated. Truthfully, my wife and I had developed few relationships outside of the teens and their parents and wanted to spend more time with those in our own age group. However, we did not feel we could take time away from the grind of youth ministry programming.

Our leaders took the decision away from us and, in a very real sense, saved and revitalized our youth ministry. They gifted us with friendship.

By the way, thirty years later, one of those leaders still checks in with my wife and me, holding us accountable to spending time with our friends and family.

TRUTH: FRIENDSHIP MATTERS

SERVING MATTERS

Your Youth Minister Cannot Do Everything nor Do Everything Well. You Have Skills and Abilities That Can Enhance Your Youth Ministry.

For the first five years of my youth ministry, I (Walter) had exactly that mindset—that it was *my* youth ministry. Not just my responsibility but *mine*. So when parents came up to me and asked how they could help, my knee-jerk reaction was, "It's OK, I've got this." I mean, that was what the church was paying me for. Right?

As a result, not only did it stretch my limits of time, energy, and resources, but I did a lot of things that were average or below average *at best*. I'd missed the point completely.

The youth ministry is not mine; it is a ministry of the church. It is *ours*.

It is important to note that right before Jesus left this fledgling movement in the hands of the apostles, "he got up from the meal, took off his outer clothing, and wrapped a towel around his waist. After that, he poured water into a basin and began to wash his disciples' feet, drying them with the towel that was wrapped around him" (John 13:4–5). Perhaps the most important lesson Jesus gave at one of the most critical moments in his ministry was the message, "It's not just my ministry but *ours*."

TRUTH: SERVING MATTERS

WHY?

What we overlook often when we read this passage is that "Jesus knew that the Father had put all things under his power, and that he had come from God and was returning to God" (John 13:3). Did you catch that? Jesus had *everything* under his power and what does he choose to do? Serve. I do not know about you, but if I had the power of the universe at my disposal, I would probably go to Italy, not wash other people's feet. Jesus knew that one of the most critical aspects of this movement was that of service.

When I thought of the youth ministry as "mine," I missed several critical aspects of Jesus's example here:

> *Everyone can serve.* Jesus is doing one of the most menial tasks, something anyone could do: wash feet. He did not choose some elaborate project requiring expertise; he chose washing feet. There are dozens of ways a parent can "wash feet" in youth ministry. I remember one parent who was a silent presence at many youth group events. He would quietly pick up trash and empty it after potlucks and lock-ins. His expertise was in designing computer chips for Intel, and here he was, taking out the trash.

> *Serving is communal.* After he's washed everyone's feet, Jesus says, "Now that I, your Lord and Teacher, have

65

washed your feet, you also should wash one another's feet" (John 13:14). Jesus, their teacher, is not only serving his apostles but passing on that expectation to them. His imperative, "you should also wash one another's feet," is an illustration of how they are to serve one another. Furthermore, it is a call to serve others. Jesus knows that serving is a marked characteristic of the Kingdom of God. I recall one set of parents who regularly opened their home for the youth group to use for meetings and also actively participated by planning what we would do when we gathered. Students quickly adopted them as surrogate parents because of the community that was naturally built through their service.

Serving is familial. Christ's example here puts the spotlight on the fact that Jesus deflects his power and is inclusive of those around us. Rather than saying, "Since I am your Lord and Teacher, you should serve others," Jesus communicates that we are to serve by doing so himself. When asked to serve in the youth ministry, I have had many parents use the excuse, "I want to give my son/daughter their space in youth ministry." This excuse is akin to saying, "I cannot serve because I am a parent," which is the opposite of Jesus's example here. Instead, he is challenging us to lay whatever titles we have down. My response to parents is that our youth ministry is big enough for you to keep your distance while providing a powerful example for your teen at the same time.

Serving is commanded. Let us let you in on a common frustration of many youth ministers. That frustration is the "drop-off" parent. "Drop-off" parents utilize the youth group as a service that is provided by the church. It is free babysitting, if you will. Perhaps this is indicative of the resistance to service many feel. Isn't it interesting that Jesus knew that his example of foot washing was not going to be sufficient and that he had to command us to wash others' feet?

HOW?

People generally are hesitant to volunteer to serve in the youth ministry because they picture it as teaching a Bible class in front of forty-five high school students onstage. While "onstage" is one way in which people can serve, it is not generally the biggest area of need. There are two others where parents are much needed that do not require the level of skill or commitment that being "onstage" does.

Front of House Service

In theaters and restaurants, "front of house" is the part of the venue that is open to the public. It is the place where the atmosphere is first experienced. For example, in a restaurant, it is the hostess stand where you are greeted and welcomed. In a theater, it is the ticket booth. Front of house is where you are generally directed to where you are to go (your table, your seat, etc.).

In youth ministry, front of house is that place of first contact. The door to the youth room can be very intimidating. I had a volunteer once who was a septuagenarian. She came to me one day and said, "I can't teach a Bible class, but I can welcome students to class." She would stand at the (open) door to the youth room and give them hugs, call them by their names, and let them know they were important. After class began, she would then go on to her own Bible class. It wasn't important that she was in class with the students or even leading a small group; what *was* important was that she was there every week to welcome each student by name. This service didn't take any special skills, just a heart to care for teens:

> *"Check-in person" for events.* As the youth minister, I spent time making sure everyone at an event was there, that we had their permission slips, had collected their fees, and so on. I was not able to be mentally present to welcome students and "be there" with them until after the event began. Having parents serve not only frees up the youth minister to minister; it gives parents an easy way to show they care about teens. Having many different faces to welcome students to an event is important to developing a culture that cares for teens.
>
> *Next level:* View this job as the ministry of hospitality. In other words, use it as an opportunity not only to check in the students and get the necessary details from them like permission slips and registration fees but to let the teens know that they are seen.

> *Drivers.* Parents can provide an invaluable service by driving on a trip or for an event. Think of how scary and intimidating boarding a church van can be for a teen unfamiliar with youth group. You can provide an invaluable ministry by being a friendly face welcoming students on the vehicle and telling them how glad you are that they are there.

Next level: Take the service of driving to the next level by being intentional, making sure different people sit "shotgun" so you ask them about their story. View your ministry not only as a driver but as a person of contact.

Backstage Service

In the theater, backstage is where props are stored, costume changes occur, sets are held, and actors prepare for their next scenes. This is the place where an inordinate amount of support happens. Without these people and responsibilities, things onstage just do not happen. While generally not seen by the larger public, it is noticed when things in the back of the house are not working. There are a wide variety of ways parents can serve backstage.

Administration/communication. Let us be honest and recognize that many youth ministers do not possess the necessary administrative skills to keep a youth ministry running smoothly. I know many parents whose day jobs keep them deep in Excel spreadsheets, budget planning, accounting, logistics, and so on. These skills can provide much-needed administrative support to a youth minister.

Technology support. A great backstage area is providing technical support for different areas of the youth ministry. This can be building and running slides for PowerPoint, mixing the worship band sound, managing youth group socials, or administering the youth group database.

Cooking. This is one area where there are numerous needs in a youth ministry. It includes not only cooking at an event but planning a menu, making the grocery list, purchasing the groceries, and preparing meals. Many parents are gifted at filling this role. This frees up other volunteers, and the youth minister, to attend to other aspects of the event.

Curriculum writing/researching. One of the great resources found in many churches is the abundance of those gifted at writing and those with a background in education. Parents can assist by evaluating curricula to see if they are developmentally appropriate for your youth ministry.

Praying. I have saved the most important backstage service for last: prayer. Perhaps the most important thing you can do as a parent in youth ministry is pray:

* Pray for your youth minister.
* Pray for your youth minister's spouse.
* Pray for your youth minister's family.
* Pray for each student in the youth group by name.
* Pray for the volunteers in the youth ministry.
* Pray for the different events coming up in the youth group in the next few weeks.
* Pray for your own children in the youth group.
* Pray for God to bring other teens to youth group.
* Pray for the schools represented in your youth ministry.
* Pray for each student in the youth group by name. I know we already said this, but this is really important.

Pick *one* to pray for each day.

The backstage of youth ministry is a vital area to which parents can bring tremendous value. Take a minute to think about all the backstage service in your youth ministry. How would things work out without this service?

Onstage Service

Finally, we would be remiss if we did not mention the more visible aspects of youth ministry: the stage. This is the area that terrifies most parents. It is also the area many people think of when they are asked to volunteer. We know that public speaking is one of the most common fears people possess. However, think about the different ways having a variety of voices speaking into the lives of young people benefits youth ministry:

> *A variety of voices meets varied needs.* I remember hearing the story of a mom as she spoke to our teens one summer. She told her story of being "spiritually single." This meant she went to church and her husband chose not to attend with her and the rest of the family. I looked around the room and noticed how many different families were in a similar situation. I thought there was never any way I could teach about the challenges such a situation presents a person. I think also about a dad in our youth ministry telling his story. This was a dad who was as straightlaced and "geeky" as they come. He shared his checkered past from college. A past that included extensive drug use and a challenging journey to find Christ. The room was floored because they could not believe it. I couldn't believe it! Afterward, I thought about the different ways students would now think about the power of Jesus's redemptive work in the lives of people.

A variety of voices meets different students. When your youth ministers take the stage to teach, only a certain percentage of students will connect with them due to their personalities, interests, hobbies, and styles. If your youth minister is doing 80–90 percent of the teaching, then your youth ministry is, at best, reaching 30–50 percent of your students. However, when parents and other volunteers take the stage, a different style of teaching and different interests will hit a different subsection of the youth ministry, creating a more effective culture of learning.

As a parent, here are a few of the ways you can serve "onstage":

Teaching. You don't have to do a thirteen-week series on the Pentateuch with an emphasis on the conjugation of Hebrew verbs. Helping one week here or there is a great way to bring different perspectives and voices to the teaching:

- Share your testimony of how you came to know Jesus.
- Talk about your history with the church.
- Tell of some of the successes and failures along your walk with Jesus.
- Teach on your favorite verse of the Bible.

Small group leaders. It is well recorded in adolescent spirituality research that for teens, having adults who care for and *know* them is one of the greatest indicators that their faith will endure as they emerge into adulthood.[1] One of the most effective ways youth ministry does this is through small groups, where closer relationships are possible.

Worship leaders. Maybe you play guitar, piano, or bass or you love to sing. Serving in your youth ministry as part of a band or helping teach students how to be part of a worship band are great ways to utilize your gifts and talents onstage.

NOW?

We just gave you several different ways to serve in your youth ministry. What now?

Warning!

Some of you are going to want to volunteer for all these positions the moment you put this book down. Please don't! We do not want you to burn yourself out. Pick one idea. Pick one that you are passionate about and pray about how you will serve in that way. Then text or email your youth minister with your idea.

Caution!

Just because you want to teach does not mean you will get to the first time you call your youth ministers. More than likely, if they take their work seriously, they will work to find the correct stage for your skill level. Don't be offended; it's their job.

Finally, know that whatever you do—whether it is in the front of house, backstage, or onstage—it matters. God will use you to reach students directly or indirectly. Your service is the physical manifestation of Jesus in the midst of teens' lives.

One of the parents, who I (Walter) will call Mike, was this type of servant. Mike did not have the kind of personality that one generally thinks of when you hear "youth group volunteer." He wasn't a twentysomething hipster who listened to the top tracks on Spotify. His wardrobe came from JCPenney, not rue21. He was better at math than he was at video games.

But Mike had a servant heart.

After every event—and I mean *every* event—that Mike was at, he was the one emptying the trash cans and taking the bag out to the dumpster. I never asked him. He just did it.

When we needed volunteers for small group leaders, Mike came forward humbly and said he could do it. Sure, I was hesitant. But you know what? Mike was a good small group leader. He was present. He was always prepared. He cared. He served, and because of that, he provided our ministry with a powerful witness to what servant leadership looks like. He definitely impacted my life.

TRUTH: SERVING MATTERS

PARTNERSHIP
MATTERS

**Your Youth Minister Doesn't Want to Do Ministry Alone
or Take Your Job as a Parent. Really!
Your Youth Minister Wants a Partnership.**

I (David) keep a picture of me and Jim carrying a pink toilet out of a hurricane-damaged house on my phone. Strange? Perhaps. The toilet-carrying moment, forever caught in time, represents one of the most difficult and crazy short-term mission experiences we ever participated in together. More than that, it is a symbol of deep, dependable, and ongoing partnership in youth ministry.

Yes, we partnered in carrying a toilet out of a hurricane-destroyed home, but . . .

    . . . we have also partnered in parenting our own, and other, students.

    . . . we have also partnered in praying for each other's struggles and pain.

. . . we have also partnered in working through each
other's loss and grief.

. . . we have also partnered in burying his beloved wife.

Jim, parent-volunteer extraordinaire, is a friend. A friend I can
call at any time of the day or night to get an answer and receive
help. The picture, though strange, is a reminder to pray for and
keep in touch with my friend.

TRUTH: PARTNERSHIP MATTERS

WHY?

In just about every gift Bible, graduation Bible, or wedding Bible
(the ones in which you highlight a verse for the recipients), I
pick and comment on this passage of Scripture: "I thank my
God every time I remember you. In all my prayers for all of you,
I always pray with joy because of your partnership in the gospel
from the first day until now, being confident of this, that he who
began a good work in you will carry it on to completion until
the day of Christ Jesus" (Phil. 1:3–6; emphasis mine). I definitely
love the "I thank God" line, but for our purposes, I am drawn
to the italicized statement. Paul described his relationship with
the Philippian church as a partnership. The word "partnership"
is *koinonia* in the original language of the letter and is probably
familiar to most readers. *Koinonia* is a frequently used word
in churches to describe the deep, abiding, committed-to-the-
struggle type of relationship held up as a model for the family
of God in the New Testament. It is a beautiful and powerful
word, one that provides a key for why parents need to partner
with their youth ministers (paid or volunteer) in order to create
a healthy youth ministry.

A *koinonia* relationship with your youth minister means . . .

. . . no matter the difficulty, you commit to working it out for the good of the whole.

. . . even when in disagreement, you commit to working toward understanding and unity.

. . . in moments when you do not *like* the youth ministers (and they may not *like* you), you commit to showing one another the respect that *love* demands.

. . . when differences and/or failure lead to a dismissal, the separation is done with honesty, straight talk, and appropriate care for the future of the youth minister (i.e., adequate severance and/or mentoring assistance).

I can hear it: "Why should I give such 'partnership' to the youth minister who I feel is a bad fit for our program and my child? I wasn't on the committee that hired her." The answer is, *Koinonia* demands that a deep, abiding, committed-to-the-struggle opportunity be given to your youth minister.

Listen, no hire is perfect, but when partnership is practiced (as in the example of Paul and the Philippian church), a scaffold of love and support is created. A scaffolding that will have a greater and much-farther-reaching impact on the students in your ministry.

Another familiar passage that anchors the expectation of partnering with your youth minister is found in the Old Testament:

Hear, O Israel: The LORD our God, the LORD is one. Love the LORD your God with all your heart and with all your soul and with all your strength. These commandments that I give you today are to be on your hearts. Impress them on your children. Talk about them when you sit at home and when you walk along the road, when you lie down and when you get up. Tie them as symbols on your hands and bind them on your foreheads. Write them on the doorframes of your houses and on your gates. (Deut. 6:4–9)

You have heard these powerful, centering words echoed by Jesus in the New Testament and have, more than likely, sang, memorized, or spoken them in a worship assembly. This passage of Scripture was and remains a serious compass-serving instruction for the people of God. This passage has a great deal to say about why you should commit to partnering with your youth minister. Here are a few partnership-supporting takeaways:

This passage was given to the entire community of God's people. It was inclusive of but not written *for* parents. Significance: It is both the parents' and youth ministers' job to support and promote spiritual health.[1] Conclusion: Partnership matters.

This passage supports the importance of having an immersive, fully devoted environment of adults involved in a student's spiritual formation. Significance: A parent cannot drop off their student to the youth ministry thinking adequate, spiritual formation will take place. It does take a village to raise a spiritually mature student.[2] Conclusion: Partnership matters.

This passage supports the truth that spiritual formation is both taught to *and* caught by *students, primarily, from the surrounding community of adults.* Significance: All adults directly or indirectly involved in youth ministry "programming" are influential in a student's spiritual formation.[3] Conclusion: Partnership matters.

In our context as professors, we have taught (actually, demanded) that young youth ministers view their job as a partnership with parents in the spiritual formation of teenagers. As parents, you must view them as partners as well. Actually, partnership is a key ingredient for imparting long-term, dynamic, and disciple-producing faith in students.

HOW?

There has been, and may continue to be in your context, a lot of pressure placed on you as a parent to be the lone responsible factor in your student's spiritual development. While, primary for sure, remember, as demonstrated above, that other adult believers play a significant role as well. Breathe! Thank the Lord he has given parents a community to help spiritually form our children. Whether fresh out of college or veteran, married or single, with kids of their own or no kids, your youth ministers are some of those partners. Here're a few ways to develop and strengthen that partnership.

Commit to a "With Mindset"

We train youth ministers to be partners *with* adults. Consider them cultural missionaries who are able to assist you in speaking "teen" with your student. Do they know everything about raising a teenager? No. If they have teenagers, they may know a little. But as we know as parents, we don't know much. Either way, they know a lot about adolescent culture. Commit to a "with mindset" when approaching youth ministry.

Understand Youth Ministry as a "Shared Key" Rather Than a "Turnkey"

Youth ministry is a shared key ministry. We train youth ministers to realize that parents and a student's surrounding adult group are his or her main influencers of spirituality. Youth ministers may be part of a student's adult group, but most are at best a distant third, after parents and surrounding adults, on the spiritual influence list.[4] Why does this matter? As parents, you may think of youth ministry programming as something of a drop-off dry cleaner.[5] Drop off your kids "wrinkled" and get them back "clean and pressed" after youth group.[6] But youth ministry is not turnkey! The parent and minister both have keys of responsibility.

Practice Collaboration and Support over Domination and Demand

Even if you needed to hear this hard truth, this suggestion should be self-explanatory. Just in case, though, I will say that as parents, we have an awful reputation for dominating and demanding when our kids are involved. Strong church leaders know how to navigate such challenges and work toward a collaborative and supportive solution to disagreements. Weak church leaders interested in peace (making everyone happy) over mission (in which people will not always be happy) give in to vocal, dominating, and demanding parents. If you are that dominating, demanding parent, how is it going for you? You may have come out the victor, but what did it cost you? What did it cost your student? When possible, practice collaboration and support. If you really feel that domination and demand are needed, be sure it is a mountain worth dying on, because there will be battle wounds and injuries.

Support the Vision of the Youth Ministry

We train youth ministers to articulate the mission and vision (the *why*) of their youth ministry programming. In other words, youth ministers do not simply pick random events to fill space on the church calendar. Furthermore, they have been taught how to develop their mission and vision in collaboration with key leaders, parents, and students. Why is this important? When your student enters the youth ministry at church, you should clearly know the expectation of and for each student, parent, volunteer, and participant at each programmed activity. If you have questions about the vision, ask the youth minister (practicing collaboration and support). If you can't support the vision of the youth ministry, you have a decision to make. That decision can be made by having an open, honest conversation (in which you are committed to having a "with mindset," one that understands youth group as a shared key, collaborative, and supportive ministry). Hear this: there is more than one way to program a youth ministry for the successful discipleship of students. Furthermore, youth ministry programming will, more than likely, look nothing like the kind you experienced as a student (see the introduction). Support your youth ministry's vision or move to a ministry you can support.

Look for Ways to Provide Relief and Support to Your Minister and Family

Do you really want to partner with your youth minister? This suggestion is imperative. If you say things like "I wish I had a job that would let me spend a week up in the mountains" to your youth minister after the group returns from a week at church camp, stop it! If you instead welcome your youth minister with "Thank you for all you are doing for my student and those in this ministry!" and hand him or her a gift card to a local restaurant, keep it up! Offering to teach classes, providing free babysitting, mowing their yards, giving gift cards, and so on are all relief-giving, supportive activities. But the greatest way to show your support and provide relief is with a word (spoken or handwritten) of appreciation for the time your youth ministers spend with your students. It's simple and powerful.

NOW?

The quickest way to end this chapter is by encouraging each of us to "get to partnering," but let me suggest another motivating exercise.

Think back to your days as a teenager. Think about what made the greatest impact on your spiritual development:

* How many programs do you remember (sermons, classes, devotionals, camps, mission trips, etc.)?
* How many adults, those who deeply impacted your spiritual development, do you remember?

Hopefully, family members made the second list. Regardless, I am certain there were significant adults on your list (including probably your youth minister). I am also fairly certain, because it is usually the case, that the list of names came more quickly than memories of the programming. Why? Partnership matters! It matters a great deal.

Now, get to partnering with your youth minister.

❋

"Do you remember when we . . . ?" are some of my favorite words to hear from parents who served with me (David) in youth ministry.

Recently, a teary parent came into my office to make plans for an adult son's funeral. Killed in a tragic accident, the conversation was, obviously, sad and difficult. Then the reminiscing started: "Do you remember when we . . . ?"

Tears turned to laughter.

Sorrow turned to joy.

Despair turned to hope for the future.

TRUTH: PARTNERSHIP MATTERS

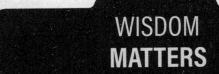

WISDOM
MATTERS

How the Past Helps Us Navigate the Present.
Drawing upon a Great Cloud of Witnesses.

A couple that I (Walter) will call John and Mary are perhaps the wisest parents I ever knew. I told myself countless times, "When I grow up, I want to be like them." I meant that.

Mind you, they were far from perfect. They had made their fair share of mistakes, and it showed, but what they lacked in perfection, they made up for in wisdom.

There were times when they looked like every other family.

There were times when they went against the grain of what was popular in their parenting.

There were times when others gathered around them.

There were times when many thought they were the second coming of Mike and Carol Brady.

I think you know why I wanted to be like these people. It was their wisdom. Something I aspire to give to others.

TRUTH: WISDOM MATTERS

WHY?

For centuries the church was society's timekeeper. You still see remnants of this today—most vividly in the liturgical calendar. The ebb and flow of the calendar from Advent to Easter and then the journey through ordinary time.

Visit an old church on the East Coast or in Europe and you will undoubtedly see the graveyard next door. Creepy? Perhaps. These tombstones and graves serve as visual reminders that we are here today because of the belief and work of these people. They were the ones who passed the faith on from generation to generation. It is the body of knowledge and their wisdom that the church relies on today. However, there was a time when the past was revered far more than it is today. The past is where the church looked for wisdom and guidance to navigate the present. The writer of Hebrews refers to this idea when it talks about being "surrounded by a great cloud of witnesses" (Heb. 11, 12). All Saints Day is a reminder of that "great cloud of witnesses" who have gone before us.

Today is much different. Some suggest that the keeper of time is no longer the church but Silicon Valley. No, not because of smart watches, but because it is the overseer of what is "new." Pay attention to the number of people in your life who are drawn to every Apple announcement made for the next "brand-new" iPhone. Even when nothing is really "new" about the phone, the excitement draws significant attention. Think about the number of emerging social media apps that have the same function as the previous apps but, because they are "new," gain our attention.[1] Time is no longer measured by the past but by what is *next*.

With the advent of technology, one might suggest that the present is actually governed by the future. What is new? What is next? What is coming? Where is my next vacation? What is my next promotion? How many likes will this post get? We are more future-focused than ever. By the way, this is the water your teen swims in daily, hourly, and even in this moment.

Why is this important to understand? Remember how the writer of Hebrews tells us about the "great cloud of witnesses" that surrounds us. Let me let you in on a terrifying secret: "You are part of this great cloud of witnesses." Yup! It's true. It is your wisdom, knowledge, and experience that the Spirit uses to help pass the faith from one generation to the next.

One of the best pieces of wisdom that got me through many years of parenting was the following:

Until I had a child, I had never been the parent of one child.

Until I have my second child, I had never been the parent of two children.

Until my children reached adolescence, I had never been the parent of two teenagers.

Until my teens left the house, I had never been the parent of two emerging adults.

See what is going on here? A significant part of parenting is literally flying blind. And we are building the airplane while in flight. However, God has designed life in such a way that as we navigate it, we generally pick up the different bits of wisdom that we need to successfully mature and grow.

Parent involvement in youth ministry is an invaluable resource that brings a wealth of wisdom to the ministry. I once was consulting with a youth ministry search team, and they were debating between two different, final candidates. One candidate was a single person. The other was a young married person with a child. Both were very qualified and brought their own set of strengths to the table. They would have hired both if they could, but resources were not there.

I made a comment that helped them decide.

Here is what I said: "I gained a certain set of skills and knowledge living on my own during college and grad school. When I got married, I developed another set of skills and knowledge that I never would have as a single person. When God gave me a child, I developed even more skills and knowledge that I didn't have as just a married person. When God gave me a second child, yet a new set of skills was developed." And so on and so on; you get the picture. The search committee had to decide which skills, knowledge, and wisdom they needed for their particular ministry at that particular time.[2]

HOW?

I inherited a fully functioning parent committee with my second youth ministry job. They were serving before I got the job and served for all five years I was at that church. We never even thought to disband them. Why? I had hit the jackpot!

The committee was made up of a combination of parents and volunteers who had a vested interest in the youth ministry. They came from a variety of backgrounds, levels of education, and fields of work, including accounting, business, and finance. We met every three or four weeks to go over what was coming up on the calendar.

When we met, I would throw out ideas and plans for events and activities, and a member of the committee would gently ask,

"Have you considered . . . ?" This would range from, "Have you considered what that would cost?" to "Is that safe?" to "What would this look like to someone who doesn't know anything about church?" to "Can you really drive one hundred miles in an hour and a half on a Friday afternoon in Southern California?"[3]

They were bringing their wisdom to my youthful passion and vision. But the last thing they would ever do was be discouraging. They knew things, had experience in various areas of life, and brought perspectives with them that I needed to consider. They had wisdom.

They knew about some things teens need that I didn't know about.

They knew about ways to budget and finance events that I had no clue about.

They had experienced the loss of close friends and relatives that I had not yet lost.

They had experience taking students on international trips and across borders that I lacked.

They knew where a notary was when I hadn't yet thought about how we'd need one. Because of their longevity with the church, they had insights into family histories that I needed to know about.

They knew a bunch of things I did not know. They had wisdom.

Think about the ministry of Peter. Jesus knew when he called Peter that, over and over, Peter would be his impetuous self. Jesus, in his infinite wisdom, shared that wisdom patiently with Peter to help him move forward. Think about the different times Peter showed his impulsiveness:

* attempting to walk on water
* suggesting they build three altars at the transfiguration

* rebuking Jesus
* trying to tell Jesus how to wash feet
* cutting off the soldier's ear in the garden

Get the point? Time after time, Peter revealed his lack of wisdom. Peter needed space and patience to mature and gain wisdom. Jesus gave him that space. Jesus saw Peter's lack of experience and knowledge and gave him the opportunity to grow through that. Jesus even let Peter make mistakes so he could learn from those too!

Whether by formal committee or casual, faithful interaction, this is the type of role parents can play in a youth ministry.

 NOW?

Here are a few suggestions for gathering the wisdom of parents active in your youth ministry:

Create advisory boards. Develop a group of four to six parents from a variety of backgrounds to meet regularly with the youth minister regarding upcoming plans and events. Parents who have lived in the area for a long time can give input on locations, services, opportunities, and so on that are in the region without having to reinvent the wheel. Some of these advisory boards need not be long term and regular. I have gleaned much help through assembling such boards for larger, onetime events like short-term missions, ski trips, and retreats. The fact that I was asking them to only meet a few times lessened the strain on their calendar and allowed for greater availability.

Request administrative support. I can barely open Excel and add a column of numbers. However, a number of parents in my youth ministry live in Excel and actually *like* developing spreadsheets. It is no secret that many youth ministers lack some of the essential administrative skills required to keep an organization running smoothly. Be that parent!

Pool parental encouragement. One of the best things I experienced as a youth minister and a new parent was access to other parents of teenagers. Getting to be around them, learn from them, and build relationships with them created a support system that helped me and my wife navigate some of the more difficult questions of parenting. Not only that, but having their examples to watch and learn from built a library of wisdom that we were able to draw from.

Teach Adulting 101. What if you suggested, planned, and ran a night of youth ministry that focused around one practical life skill that teens need to know? Maybe it is something like basic auto maintenance, where you host a class in the parking lot, teaching teens how to check their fluids and change their oil. Maybe, because you were an English major, take an afternoon to teach teens how to write a college essay. If you are a great cook, offer to teach graduating seniors how to make a meal for themselves using only things they would find in a dorm room. You get the idea. You have a skill that the teens in your youth ministry can benefit from. Share those ideas, and desire to run with them, with your youth minister.

Hold a Night of Remembrance. To combat the future-focused perspective that drives most of our teens' lives, we hosted a Night of Remembrance every January. This was an evening we took to look back on and celebrate the work of God in our lives as a youth ministry. We ate dinner, recounted funny stories, and recognized milestones like baptisms, but most importantly, we looked at the work God had done in our lives as a church over the previous year. We reflected on the differences in our faith and looked forward to what God would do in the upcoming year.

Share summer stories. One of the richest things that the body of Christ can offer our teens in the way of wisdom is stories. Since summers are typically full of activity, making it difficult to keep a curriculum on schedule, we used open weeks to let various men and women in the church, from all different demographics, share their testimonies. Sometimes it was a couple who had been married for fifty-plus years teaching relationship advice, sometimes it was a dad from our youth ministry sharing his story of wandering during his years in college, sometimes it was a "spiritually single" mom talking about the journey of doing faith without a believing spouse. Powerful wisdom was shared in a series of one-off classes. Maybe you can be one of those stories or you can be the one who helps develop the panel of speakers for a summer and take that off your youth minister's to-do list.

Look to the liturgical calendar. If you are part of a tradition that doesn't adhere to the liturgical calendar, consider borrowing from the wisdom of those that have gone before us by incorporating the rhythm of the liturgical calendar. The lectionary takes the church through reading, teaching, and preaching the entire Bible over the course of three years, forcing us to look beyond the passages we like the best.

There is likely one area of your life, Christian walk, and/or parenting that you have a bit of wisdom-filled insight into. Think of a way to incorporate that into your youth ministry. Now approach your youth minister with your desire to share that wise insight.

Yes, it can be scary getting in front of teenagers. Yes, you might doubt the value of what you have to share. Work through that fear. Your wisdom is a necessary part of the body of Christ, and your teens need to learn from you.

"When I was eighteen years old, my husband was murdered, leaving me as a young mother with a newborn baby." Once these words were spoken, you could have heard a pin drop.

The senior saint had the attention of over 250 high school students, each waiting to hear how she navigated such a horrific and challenging situation with her faith intact. She spoke as part of an ongoing series, Stories of Faith, in my (David's) youth ministry.

Can senior church members actually impact and be welcomed onto the youth ministry stage?

Absolutely!

Wisdom was shared.

TRUTH: WISDOM MATTERS

DISCIPLESHIP
MATTERS

Taking Others to the Places You Have Been Yourself.
Being a Spiritual Trail Guide.

I (Walter) have been on a number of difficult hikes all over the world. Perhaps the most difficult journey I have ever been on was a day-long hike in Peru to the archaeological site Llaqtapata. The day started before sunrise with a four-to-five-mile, mostly uphill hike. Thankfully, my guide, Emilio, knew the way. He would point out flora and fauna that I would have otherwise missed. He knew to give us coca leaves to chew to fight off possible altitude sickness. He even knew where we could get a cup of coffee from a family who ran a remote business out of their house hidden deep in the mountains. He showed us beautiful and inviting plants we should avoid at all costs, because they are poisonous. He shared the history of the region to give our journey more depth and significance. Finally, after five hours of strenuous hiking, we arrived at Llaqtapata, which translated literally means "elevated place." Llaqtapata is about three miles west of Machu Picchu, so once you arrive at this former fortress city, you are greeted with a sweeping panoramic view of Machu Picchu as well as the Inca Trail. It figuratively and literally (because of the hike and altitude) takes your breath away. It truly is an "elevated place."

Because of the amount of work it takes to get there, there are not many who get to see such an amazing site. I was fortunate enough to have an experienced and trustworthy guide. There is no way I could have traveled the path to Llaqtapata safely or successfully by myself. And even though we then also had a four-hour-long hike to get back home, it was a journey worth making.

The process of discipleship has a lot of parallels. It helps to have guides who have traveled to places we hope to go ourselves. They know the way. Guides tell us what to pay attention to on the path and what to avoid. Guides give us the encouragement to keep putting one foot in front of the other when we no longer want to move. And when we arrive at the overlook, we take in the view together, as peers.

TRUTH: DISCIPLESHIP MATTERS

WHY?

The church is one of the only, if not the only, organizations that exist for those who are not yet a part of it. Its mission is to make disciples, as we are reminded in the Great Commission. Perhaps one of the most important places that this discipleship happens is within the home and the family. By operating for decades as a separate entity from the larger body of the church, youth ministry has probably cut itself off from significant discipling opportunities. What if the church embraced this mission of discipleship and saw the next generation as the most important ministry to devote itself to?

And what if parents embraced their roles in youth ministry as well?

But what if my teen does not want me at youth group? This is a common refrain we have heard from parents for our entire careers. While on the surface, that may appear to be the case, research shows the best chance for students to continue on in the faith occurs when parents take up their role as the primary influencers of spiritual formation in the lives of their teens.[1] Volunteering in youth group is one way to do so.

Won't I be just crowding my teen's space? In our experience, youth group is big enough for parents to have their own space and influence. We follow this up with asking that parent to think about the impact they are having on their own teenagers from a distance. Think about how having your own teen seeing you involved in various aspects of youth group is a means of formation and discipleship.

The beauty of a healthy youth ministry is that it is an open space that allows parents to come in and be mentors and examples to the other teens in the youth group as well.

I think about Kevin, who was a mountain of a man. He stood over six feet and worked on cars. He cherished his own days growing up in youth group and loves volunteering in youth ministry now, finding ways for other teens to enjoy church. Kevin has two daughters. I am sure if they were asked if they minded that their dad participated in their youth group, their initial response would have been less than enthusiastic. However, Kevin came and jumped in to volunteer. Due to his interest in restoring cars, service on the praise team, and love of the band U2, he attracted students that I could never have impacted. He also did it far away from his daughters. He never got up in their space.

You might say that Kevin was discipling his daughters indirectly. His model of serving and being faithful provided for them a vivid picture of what it means to be an adult Christian servant in the church.

Disciples make disciples who make disciples.

HOW?

You might think that discipling entails having daily, hour-long Bible studies at the breakfast table before school or hosting prayer meetings every Thursday night before bed. We are not sure what it is, but there is this fear that discipleship is this long, arduous series of intentional activities that require expert skills and involved training. However, the most important lesson of discipleship is just showing up and sharing space in a student's life.

Showing up is 80 percent of ministry. Being there matters. When you as a parent not only come to church but become active members of the faith community, discipleship happens through your example for your children at exponentially high rates.

We probably need to be clear about what we mean when we say "active members." Our experience tells us that for a few decades, an active member was one who just came to church on Sundays. While this is important, we don't consider this to be an accurate description of what it means to be "active."

Theologically, a member of a church is one who does in fact show up but also actively participates in ministry. Perhaps church leadership has been a bit timid in speaking up about this second characteristic. Perhaps leadership has relied too much on people simply showing up. You are probably familiar with the statistic that 80 percent of the ministry in a church is done by 20 percent of the members. While we would love for you to be actively involved in youth ministry, we understand that not everyone is cut out for that. But imagine what kind of impact your example would have on your son or daughter if, week after week, they know you are serving in the first grade class, or leading a small group of fifth graders, or serving on the worship team?

Personally, one of the most vivid memories I have of my father before he left was the one Sunday he was asked to help with the collection at church. Seeing him pass the offering plate gave me tremendous pride, knowing that was my dad. I often wonder how I would be different if I had witnessed such service, year after year, from my dad.

Sadly, all too often, there is this great divide created when teens and adults go off to their separate worlds, only to be seen together in very rare instances in church, school, extracurricular activities, and culture in general. As a result, Chap Clark observes that the result is the "systematic abandonment of adolescents."[2] Teens are left up to fend for themselves, to navigate all the perils and pitfalls of adolescence alone. Youth culture has been created through the vacuum created by adults leaving their posts to mentor and disciple teens through adolescence into adulthood. Only recently have some of those divisions been reconciled.

Fictive Kin: Parents Aren't the Only Disciplers

Fictive kin is a term that ethnographers use to describe social bonds that form between those who are not biologically or legally connected to you. These are those people who you might call "Aunt" or "Uncle" even though they are not legally or bio-logically related to you. The Bible has its own terms for fictive kin: brother or sister in Christ. This is one of the strengths of being part of a church community. We are surrounded by those spiritual aunts and uncles, brothers and sisters. The writer of Hebrews talks about the "great cloud of witnesses" (Heb. 12:1) that surround each of us. Sociologists speak of the importance, both positively and negatively, these fictive kin relationships play in the lives of teens. Teens who have had fictive kin in their lives who are actively involved in the church are more likely to stay involved in the community into adulthood.[3] Moreover, fictive kin provide vital relational connections that encourage greater participation in the life of the church for those teens who do not have believing parents.

Disciple Making Is a Team Sport

For years, the magic ratio that youth workers strove for was 1:5. We wanted to have one adult for every five teens present in youth group programing in order to have enough coverage. What research is showing is the need to reverse that ratio. Instead of a 1:5 ratio, we are striving for a 5:1 ratio. By this, we don't mean there should be thirty adults at youth group with six teens in attendance. That would just be weird. Instead, what we mean is that every teen in youth group should have five adults they know and who know them well. Do they have five people they can point to and say, "He has my back" or "I can go to her"?

How do you become one of those five?

* Volunteer at one event a semester.
* Show up at the beginning of class and say, "Hi!" to teens you know.

* Lead a small group of eighth graders.
* Go to camp or the fall retreat.
* Learn the teens' names in youth group.
* Say hi to the teens you know at church.
* Become a driver for events.
* Engage two teens a week in conversation after church.
* Periodically teach class.
* Cook at events and talk to the teens you see there.
* Talk to the teens whose parents are in your adult small group.

You can see there are a variety of levels of involvement. Some of these require more effort and time than others, but all build relationships with teenagers. Note that some of these suggestions, like teaching, will need to be worked out with your youth ministers. Remember, you may not be gifted and/or needed for upfront service. However, as you will find out, most relationships with teenagers rarely happen because of an "onstage" moment. Simple, authentic interaction is best.

 ## NOW?

Here's how you can move forward:

> *Take others to your own Llaqtapatas.* Discipleship is a journey filled with a variety of destinations. There are only so many destinations that I have traveled to. Therefore, as a youth minister, it was imperative for me to gather a team around me who had been to other destinations. Destinations like those they'd reached after surviving a serious illness, growing through a long-term marriage, moving states, going through a divorce, and facing the death of a loved one I may not have in

my own faith journey. I couldn't serve as a spiritual, experienced guide for students facing those challenges. But others could. You can set up signposts along the paths you have taken to guide others in their journey.

Help someone get from Point B to Point B.5. I have a friend who was intimidated by the idea of discipleship and evangelism because of the enormous responsibility she put upon herself for such a task. She had the idea that if you begin the discipleship process with a person, it was your responsibility to see it through to the end. Instead of seeing discipleship as a multistep process, where she could assist a teen from point A to point B, she thought it was her responsibility to carry a student to point Z. It took a lot of time to help her see her responsibility is merely to help whomever she is working with move to the next point. And even if that person made it halfway to the next point, that is still progress, and she did her job as a discipler.

Go somewhere you haven't been before. It is important for you to push and challenge yourself in your own journey as a disciple. I remember early in my ministry, I was working on a camp with a few mentors who were talking about their practices of fasting. I had not been given any formal training on fasting either in seminary or in the churches I had been part of and was curious. I began asking them over a dozen questions about fasting. I asked why they fasted, how they fasted, and how long they fasted. I was then faced with a decision. What would I do with this newfound information? Would I go somewhere I had never gone before and practice fasting? Honestly, I didn't want to take this step. I was scared. I wasn't sure what it would be like to go without solid food for a number of days. Would I survive? Well, I did, and it deepened, and continues to deepen, my spiritual life.

My (Walter's) hike to Llaqtapata was difficult; it stretched my limits. At times, I didn't think I could make it another step, but I did. I couldn't have reached the summit without my guide, Emilio.

As a result, I was greeted with an entirely new perspective on my relationship with Christ. Because the same is true of my spiritual journey: I don't think I could have ever reached this point if I didn't have guides in my life who had gone before me, patiently answering my dozens of questions.

We need guides. We need disciples who know how to disciple.

TRUTH: DISCIPLESHIP MATTERS

PARENTING MATTERS

Do What God Calls You to Do as a Parent. That Helps Your Youth Minister More Than Almost Anything Else.

My wife was volunteering at our children's camp one summer many years ago when she overheard a very interesting and revealing conversation between a mother and her daughter. The mother was letting her daughter know that this was the last year she would be at camp with her, since next year the daughter would be attending the middle school camp and "they don't let parents go to camp."

Completely untrue. Not sure where she heard that. Not sure if that was messaging that had been fabricated or completely misunderstood. Actually, the opposite is true. We desperately needed parents at camp for the very reasons we will talk about in this chapter.

But my wife thought, "How tragic and sad. What a missed parenting opportunity."

In my (Walter's) early days of youth ministry, there was this myth that parents were the enemy of the youth ministry.

If you were to survey some of the *Youthworker Journals* and *Group Magazines* of the 1990s, you would see a number of cartoons and articles that would take cheap shots at parents as the enemy in youth ministry. There was also other subtle messaging that propagated the misnomer that teens don't want their parents around. To be fair, youth ministry was probably only mirroring similar messaging prevalent in pop culture. But none of it is true.

TRUTH: PARENTING MATTERS

 WHY?

If you calculate the number of hours a typical youth minister has to influence a teen, throughout any given year, you would be lucky to get upwards of a hundred hours. And that's if your son or daughter goes to youth group and small groups twice a week for most of the year and then goes to camps, retreats, and a few youth group activities. One hundred hours. That's it! Two and a half weeks of influence.

However, if you add up the number of hours parents have to influence their kids in a given year, that number jumps to about three thousand hours.

Three. Thousand. Hours. Of. Influence.

This includes both the direct and indirect influence you have on your son or daughter. So as a mom or a dad, *you* are the one who has the most influence on your student. You are the most important spiritual director in your teenagers' lives. Not their youth pastors. Not their small group leaders. Not the college interns. You.

Don't get us wrong. The youth pastors, volunteers, small group leaders, and interns are all wonderful people who play their particular roles in reinforcing what you are doing in your home. However, no one can out-parent your influence.

HOW?

OK. We admit, it is rather intimidating and frightening to realize you are the greatest spiritual influence in your student's life. We know; we are parents of teenagers. We should never take this responsibility lightly, but we do not want you to feel over-whelmed. Being a great influence is not about perfection but intentionality and authenticity. With that in mind, here are a few suggestions for strengthening your spiritual influence on your own student.

Take Care and Protect Your Faith

This stands at the forefront of any recommendations for influencing your student's spiritual life and needs little expansion. We followed our parents' leads, and your student will follow yours. This truth has been directly spoken to and/or implied throughout this book. We cannot state this more strongly: Your student is watching you! They don't expect perfection, but they should expect willful, committed, faithful direction.

Take Care and Protect Your Marriage

We know you love your teen. We also know that you love your spouse. However, one of the brutal realities of the adolescent years is that the countless activities, homework assignments, games, and club meetings can unintentionally squeeze out the important time a husband and wife need to stay connected. The care and nurture of your marriage is the best thing you can do for your student and youth minister.

Be a Great Parent to Your Teens

I can count on my hand the number of times one of my parents went to a little league game, school assembly, or band concert of mine. It was a different time in the 1600s, I know. Presence is 80 percent of ministry and parenting. We get that juggling family, life, and career is difficult, but showing up is half the job.

Being a great parent entails a lot of different things like discipline, presence, passing down wisdom, teaching, and loving. The best thing you can do for your youth minister is be a great parent. Period. That way, as youth ministers, we are simply filling in some of the blanks and giving some color commentary to what is already happening at home. Hopefully, we are just echoing what you are already telling them. This is known as "convergence."

If It Is Better for Your Family, Keep Your Kids Home from Youth Group Programming

If I am being honest, before I had children of my own, I would judge families who would keep their teens home from youth group activity. Then I had my own family, and I quickly understood the arduous nature of life with children: all the homework, projects, practices, and stress. I soon found myself making some of the same Solomon-like decisions when my own daughters were teens. Do they stay home, or do I make them go to youth group? A wise parent is one who realizes that, sometimes, the best thing for your student and family is a break from all the busyness. Yes, this may include the busyness of youth group activities.

Speak Kindly of Your Youth Minister and Church Leadership (Students Are Listening)

It is a fact that your youth minister is going to make some mistakes. They will say things you do not agree with. They are going to schedule events that conflict with important family events. They may play Justin Bieber music before Bible class. We get that. What you may not think much about is *how* you voice your disagreement in the car on the way home from church.

We are not saying you have to rubber-stamp everything that your youth minister does without complaint. We are saying a good parent speaks kindly of the work and ministry that your youth pastor is doing so that your teens are able to recognize the value and importance of it. Speaking kindly about those in leadership is an important gift you can give your teens.

 NOW?

The first thing we all need to do now is commit to being reliable, spiritual influences in our own students' lives. This may begin with you *apologizing* to your student and committing to being a better example. It certainly includes *taking responsibility* for and making the most of the time the Father has given you to impact your student. Remember, youth ministers are here to assist, support, and partner with you in the spiritual upbringing of your student.

What can you do now with your youth minister's assistance, support, and partnership?

Be patient; they may never have had kids (educate them).
When we started in youth ministry, we knew everything about adolescent culture and the spiritual development of teens. Then we had children of our own, and those

children grew into teens. It was then that we realized we did not know everything, or anything, about parenting adolescents.

It took the wise counsel of patient parents walking alongside us to teach us about some of the challenges specific to raising children that our single and childless selves were clueless about.

Accept and learn to "handle" critiques of your student with openness and thankfulness. It does take a village (Deut. 6:4–9).

Understand that youth workers are cultural missionaries and may have something to teach you. When the majority of our lives are spent living in the subculture of adolescence, we begin to gain insights that a parent may not be privy to. This is where you can feel free to approach your youth minister for advice and insight. They may have some wisdom as it relates to social media, music trends, and the latest Netflix shows that are influencing your teen in particular ways.

I (Walter) came from a home of divorce.

My father left our home to start another life with his new family when I was young. I don't share that to solicit pity. There were some valuable lessons learned through many difficult nights and years growing up without a dad. One of the things I learned was the importance of parents doing what parents do. Here is what I mean.

The times I went to friends' homes and was able to see a functioning, intact family provided a picture of something

beautiful and "normal." The times I was able to eat a family dinner around a table with a healthy family gave me a desire for
something I wanted in my own life. I am certain these moms
and dads who had me around their tables didn't think what they
were doing was "youth ministry," but it was.

Here is the point: You can be a youth minister simply by
being the parent that God called you to be.

TRUTH: PARENTING MATTERS

DISCIPLINE
MATTERS

Even If We Don't Like Discipline, We All Need It. Even Your Kid!

Let me start by saying that I (David) could have handled it differently. If I had to do it over, I would have included another adult as a witness, but I didn't. That ended up being a mistake.

I had a group of young men who made life difficult for the students around them. In fact, one student was so beaten down by their joking he left their school, our youth ministry, and went to the other side of town for a new start.

I loved this group of young men and wanted the best for them (and still do). However, I was determined to put an end to their toxic interactions and make clear what my expectations were and how they would need to act if they wanted to be involved in our ministry.

They needed discipline.

There were a number of reasons this was going to be a challenge, but I really felt I could reach these young men and help them use their power positively instead. So on a youth group trip, when their bullying caused yet another upheaval in our group, I decided it was time for discipline.

I pulled the group of young men and those they'd bullied away for a "hard" conversation. I have shared tougher words and expectations, but I left feeling I had broken through to this group and expected only positive results and change upon our return home.

Wrong! What in the world could have happened? (This is where that "adult witness" I mentioned earlier would have been nice.)

Upon returning home, the ringleaders of this group of young men told their parents a fabricated version of the conversation and events leading up to the talk. Because they didn't visit with me to discuss it, the parents believed their students were being unfairly targeted by the youth ministry. I didn't know about this misunderstanding and therefore was unable to address their concerns until much later.

Needless to say, because of the lack of support from the parents concerning the discipline given, an opportunity for change was lost. This group of young men continued to have difficulty in our ministry.

TRUTH: DISCIPLINE MATTERS

WHY?

As parents, we are fairly confident embracing the importance of discipline in our own homes and work environments. Certainly, if you have ever served as a volunteer at a junior high lock-in, you know the importance of discipline. We teach new youth ministers (and some older ones) that *a disciplined environment provides emotional and physical safety*. Fostering a safe environment in a youth ministry is crucial for a student—or an adult, for that matter—to open up and explore faith. Actually, the desire for and pursuit of safe places and people is embedded in the human experience. Discipline is one of the ways safety is fostered and maintained in a youth ministry.[1]

The Bible has a lot to say about discipline. Seriously, there are a lot of verses on it! So many that I will only share my favorite Scripture on the topic: "Whoever loves discipline loves knowledge, but whoever hates correction is stupid" (Prov. 12:1).

Is that not one of the greatest scriptures ever? I do not recommend posting this one on the refrigerator door, but it cuts to the point quickly. The theological need for and purpose of discipline is easy to find in Scripture. Certainly not as harsh, this next one is one of my favorites and demonstrates the need and benefit of receiving discipline:

> In your struggle against sin, you have not yet resisted
> to the point of shedding your blood. And have you
> completely forgotten this word of encouragement that
> addresses you as a father addresses his son? It says,
>
> > My son, do not make light of the Lord's discipline,
> > and do not lose heart when he rebukes you,
> > because the Lord disciplines the one he loves,
> > and he chastens everyone he accepts as his son.
>
> Endure hardship as discipline; God is treating you as
> his children. For what children are not disciplined by
> their father? If you are not disciplined—and everyone
> undergoes discipline—then you are not legitimate,
> not true sons and daughters at all. Moreover, we have
> all had human fathers who disciplined us and we

respected them for it. How much more should we submit to the Father of spirits and live! They disciplined us for a little while as they thought best; but God disciplines us for our good, in order that we may share in his holiness. No discipline seems pleasant at the time, but painful. Later on, however, it produces a harvest of righteousness and peace for those who have been trained by it.

Therefore, strengthen your feeble arms and weak knees. "Make level paths for your feet," so that the lame may not be disabled, but rather healed. (Heb. 12:4–13)

I know, why not give the reference instead of this long section of Scripture? Honestly, I was concerned you would not stop to turn to your Bible and instead skip to the next section. If you have time, read the above Scripture again, slowly, and embrace the importance of discipline in your own life and that of your student. One of the things you will notice is that discipline is a gift, and you have a choice to make regarding how you will handle the opportunity to learn.

HOW?

Fact: the youth ministers who work with your student may or may not be married or have kids. They will not understand all that you know about discipline. However—and this is a big *however*—they will be trained (most likely coupled with practical internship experiences) and know a bit about establishing a disciplined, safe environment for class and trips. Furthermore, they may even have a theology behind their discipline that would be helpful to your understanding of the incident.[2] Still, like all of us, they will have successes and failures in the execution of expectations and discipline procedures. With this in mind, how do you support discipline in your youth ministry?

Support the Expectations of the Youth Ministry

Your youth minister should be able to clearly articulate expectations for trips, gatherings, and other programming.[3] Get behind and support those expectations. More than once, I've encountered a parent who wants special exceptions from the rules. Not because the exception was appropriate, but because their precious student does not like the rule (yes, I used *precious* on purpose). This caused unnecessary tension. If an exception is needed, have a conversation with your minister. More than likely, he or she will understand the request and work with you and your student.

Know There Is Always Another Side to the Discipline

If your student comes home upset about the discipline he or she received, take a deep breath, listen, and then reach out to the minister for the other side of the story. Again, there is always another side (or perception) of the event that led to the discipline.

Be Thankful That Someone Loves Your Student Enough to Bring the Discipline

This is a big one, friends. As a parent, I appreciate the fact that my kids have adults who care enough to call them into account and discipline them when needed. I know, I may be old school, but Deuteronomy 6:4–9 supports that old-school, it-takes-a-village mindset. It actually demands it!

If in Doubt, Ask the Youth Minister

Here is where it can get tense. What if you don't agree with the youth minister's discipline of your student? What if, as a volunteer, you don't agree with the way he or she conducts him or herself in disciplining another student? If it is possible, in private, ask the youth minister to clarify and explain the disciplinary action. Such conversation often clears up the problem. However, if you are still confused or stand in disagreement, take the next step.

If in Doubt, Ask the Supervisor of the Youth Minister

It happens. Disagreements are such that you need a third party to get involved to settle a disciplinary issue. Let's be clear: even though it's tempting, do not talk to the supervisor *before* talking to the youth minister. When this happens, trust can or will quickly be broken and cause hard-to-fix relationship problems in the future. It is best to let youth ministers know you are going to talk to their supervisors and welcome their participation in the meeting. This is a more difficult approach but will demonstrate that you want to fix a problem, not get them fired.

Include Your Student in the Process

More than likely, your youth minister will ask for or expect the participation of your student in the discipline discussion. Unless a great reason exists, don't wait for your youth minister to ask; involve your student in the meeting. Why? Your student can further clarify and/or articulate his or her side of the story. And another great benefit is that the student will witness and learn, firsthand, how followers of Christ handle disagreement.

NOW?

You are ready to support and work with your youth minister in creating and protecting a safe, disciplined environment of ministry. Here's how:

> *Decide now to accept and learn from the discipline.* It's not a matter of if, but when. Your student (and maybe you) will get "in trouble" at some point in your experience with youth ministry.

> *Don't take the discipline of your student personally.* Again, more than likely, your student will receive discipline. Can it create embarrassment for a parent? Absolutely! Remember (easier said than done), the discipline of your student should be appreciated and embraced. It is about *the student*, not *you!*[4]

> *Take a breath and stay calm.* Discipline has been handed down to your student. What now? Take a breath, stay calm, and work the program. Remember, no matter the circumstances you are facing (we acknowledge some of you may have a painful, heart-hurting road ahead of you), our Father loves your kids more than you! Reach out to the faith community. We really want to walk through this with you.

Whatever happened to that "undisciplined" group of young men?

* Difficult conversations finally happened.
* Sides of the story were communicated, heard, and understood.

* Trust was restored with students and parents.
* Lessons were learned on both sides.
* Most importantly, relationships were restored and continue to this day.

TRUTH: DISCIPLINE MATTERS

INTERNSHIPS
MATTER

Training Young Men and Women for
Future Kingdom Ministry. Preparing Interns to Be
Great Youth Minister Parents.

"You will never guess what John did!"

John (name changed to protect the guilty) was my (Walter's) intern for the summer, and we were at camp.

"What?" I asked this thirteen-ish-year-old camper from my youth ministry.

"He put a dead mouse in his mouth! A *mouse*!" he exclaimed.

"Sheesh," was my first thought.

Let me tell you a bit about John. He was a student at one of our denomination's Christian colleges who had a heart as big as can be. He had a personality and charisma to match his big heart. He was serious about his faith and loved the church. He was a hard worker, and the students in our ministry flocked to him. He was just like I've always imagined Peter to be: young and charismatic but also . . . well . . . impetuous.

Just like the management books teach, every strength is also a weakness. Right?

Don't get me wrong. I love John. John was great for our ministry. He brought an energy and availability that I did not have that summer, having two young children at home. But with youth comes the lack of wisdom and inexperience. This is the rub with internships.

Interns can provide a valuable and important service to your youth ministry. As a parent, you may be thinking, "Don't the interns work for the youth minister? What can I do?" This is what this chapter is all about.

TRUTH: INTERNSHIPS MATTER

WHY?

I think about the story in the Gospels where Jesus is teaching at the home of Mary and Martha and the squabble comes up between them about who is really doing what is right and important. There is a lot going on in this story. Martha is opening her home to Jesus: the ministry of hospitality. Mary is sitting at Jesus's feet: the ministry of learning. Jesus is presumably teaching: the ministry of education. Do you notice that Jesus doesn't rebuke Martha for her hospitality? But he does praise Mary for her choice to listen and learn. Without going too much more into the story, what we see is a number of powerful roles that can help an internship at your church. The bottom line is that this story reveals that there is always much to do in ministry, whether that be cooking, opening your home, or sitting and learning.

Let's view internships from a thirty-thousand-foot perspective by looking at the roles they can play in a church. There are a variety of reasons churches do internships:

There is more to do than one person can do. Ministry is a Sisyphean task; there are always meetings to attend, phone calls to make, emails to return, classes to prep for, and problems to address. Having more bodies on your ministry team helps tackle these needs.

Interns can help you serve more than one gender in your ministry. Churches have learned the value of having both genders represented in ministry to adolescents. They have seen that there are certain issues each gender is better suited to address.

Now, there are a variety of types of interns that are helpful to understand in order to know how to best serve your youth ministry's needs. As a parent, it is helpful to discern which type your ministry needs most:

Summer employee / hired help. When one thinks of a summer intern, this is usually the image that comes to mind. Churches hire a college student who needs extra money for school to run to Costco to get supplies for vacation Bible school and camp, make copies, help chaperone a lock-in, and so forth. These are all part of a youth minister's summer to-do list, and these things need to get done. However, if this is the only expectation they have for an intern, many ministries, churches, and families might be settling for less.

Youth-minister-in-training. Many Christian colleges and universities with campus ministry programs have dozens of students who have a calling to serve the Kingdom through full-time ministry to young people. What if your church searched for those young people to serve as your ministry interns? What would be the different experiences, knowledge, training, and skills you would want to intentionally develop in them so they could be successful in youth ministry when they graduate? How might you help intentionally develop an internship program that involves more than running errands and hanging out with teens?

Future vocational ministers. The reality is that most summer internships will not result in that full-time ministry service. That does not mean that your internship is not useful. What if your internship approached its twelve-week program as a training session for future adult volunteers, deacons, elders, and youth group parents in the church, waving the banner for the vital importance of ministry to young people? How might your internship affect the broader field of youth ministry and the Kingdom of God in five or ten years?

See how exciting your internship program can be when you think bigger than the ten or twelve weeks you have that intern at your church? When we develop a Kingdom mindset for our internships, we can really develop intern programs that are multifaceted and intentional, meeting the needs of not only your own sons and daughters but the sons and daughters of your sons and daughters decades from now!

HOW?

You might be thinking to yourself, "How can I help out with the internship program in my church?" There are a number of ways you as a parent can impact and develop a powerful internship.

Be an Advocate

Be a voice for the importance of your church participating not only in the spiritual development of the teens in your church but in the Kingdom. Whispering in the ears of deacons and elders about how your church needs an internship program is a great way to help the process.

Be a Host Family

Many internships survive on the fact that there are members who have an extra bedroom that can be used to house an intern for the summer, thus reducing the financial impact on the church. It also allows for the interns to take home more of the money they are earning for college by not having to spend it on room and board over the summer.

Be a Resource

Parents in youth ministry are a treasure trove of skills and knowledge that can enhance your internships in a variety of ways:

* You may have expertise in human resources and can help with the legal matters that affect how a church pays a summer intern legally.[1]
* You may be a deacon or elder in your church who can invite your interns into leadership meetings to give them a "behind the scenes" tour of church leadership.
* You may be a high school teacher who can mentor your interns on lesson plans for a Bible class and then give them classroom management tips after you observe them teaching your middle schoolers.

* You may be a member of the parent-teacher organization in the local school who has overseen a variety of fundraisers for your son or daughter's class. You could develop a fundraising campaign in your church to help fund a summer internship. Most internships need $3,000–$5,000.

* You might be a talented chef. What if you worked with an intern to help develop a menu for a summer event and teach your intern how to plan a meal, shop for it, and cook it? Many interns may only know how to order from GrubHub or cook a bowl of Cup Noodles and have no clue how to feed a group of ten, thirty, or seventy-five people.

* You may have the gift of encouragement. Every time I do something as simple as lead a prayer or offer a communion thought at church, I always get a short note from one of the members in our church thanking and encouraging me. Many interns are far away from home and could use your encouragement. Take them out for a coffee. Host them for a dinner and game/movie night in your home.

* You might be someone who travels a lot for work. If you have frequent-flier miles, consider donating them to your intern. A long weekend trip home halfway through an internship can help stave off homesickness.

* You may not know what to do. In that case, pray. Pray for your interns. Pray for their hearts to grow in their love of adolescents. Pray for their wisdom and knowledge to grow through this internship. Meet them at church once a week and pray *with* them. Pray

for their hearts to be protected from the cynicism that sometimes comes when one looks behind the curtain and sees the workings and politics of church.

We hope the gears in your brain are turning as you think about how you could help be an important part of your church's next summer intern program.

NOW?

Pick one place to take your interns:

Geographically? Where are some actual places you might be able to take your interns to teach them something? Maybe take them to visit one of your members who is confined to a nursing home. Maybe take them to a meeting of deacons to see how a church runs administratively. Maybe take them to Costco as you pick up supplies for vacation Bible school and show them how something like that works behind the scenes.

Socially? Who are some people in your church you could introduce to them to learn from? Maybe this means taking them to coffee with your favorite Sunday school teacher and intentionally interviewing them together to learn their stories. Maybe work with them to help make phone calls for an upcoming event. (Many emerging adults lack the social skills necessary to do something as simple to you as making an actual phone call to a stranger.)

Spiritually? Is there a place you have been spiritually that you could "guide" your interns through? Maybe it is a spiritual discipline like fasting, prayer, meditation, or solitude that you have grown from practicing. Maybe your interns just need to hear how Jesus has captured your heart and brought you to faith.

We have given you dozens of ideas that have hopefully sparked a dozen more ideas. Pick one. Don't overdo it. Just do one thing this year to make your internship just a bit better.

❀

I (David) was eighteen years old when I worked my first internship. Even though I was young, what I learned accelerated my career in youth ministry. Why? Because of the support, coaching, and correction provided by the youth minister and the families I was partnered with in ministry.

The following classic intern mistake may not seem like a big deal, but it was to my youth minister and families on the mission trip: We were eating what I will call a fancy supper at the restaurant located in our hotel when I taught the student at my table how to tell if your glass was "real" crystal.

If you know, you know: in short, I took my wet finger and ran it in circles across the top of my glass, producing a high-pitched whining sound. You guessed it: soon all the students joined in on the experiment, creating a symphony of high-pitched whining.

Needless to say, the youth minister and volunteers quickly ended the concert and, later in private, reminded me of my failure of influence and cultural witness.

Lesson learned. I have never held such a concert again, and I remember the power of my influence and cultural witness daily.

TRUTH: INTERNSHIPS MATTER

HIRING MATTERS

Fit Is Just as Important as Qualifications. Don't Cheat the Process.

"I voted for the other guy!"

These were words I (David) heard on my first day, at my first job, in my first year of youth ministry.

I have shared this in various places: these words were spoken by a teenager who is now very much grown, thriving in ministry, and a dear colleague—who, by the way, still reminds me of his vote cast over thirty years later.

The process my wife and I went through was the most thorough hiring experience I have ever been a part of in all my years of youth ministry. After the initial résumé request, follow up, and interview with the search committee (lots of people and lots of questions), we were invited to participate in a "Candidate Tryout Weekend." It was a long time ago, but here are the parts of the weekend I remember:

Saturday morning: Have breakfast with church staff.

Saturday lunch: Have a meal with the youth ministry leadership team.

Saturday night: Hang out with the youth group and families.

Sunday morning: Teach combined youth classes with families and leadership present; preach the morning sermon.

Sunday lunch: Have a meal at a local restaurant, where the leadership, students, and families ask questions.

Sunday afternoon: Go to a meeting with the elders.

Sunday afternoon: Receive evaluation and feedback from the search committee on the weekend tryout.

There were three candidate tryout weekends. At the end of the process, votes were taken and tallied. And whether by electoral college or popular vote (I like to think I won both), I received my first job offer. Considering the student's comment on day one, I am guessing the popular vote was close.

Because of the problems that can arise in this weekend-tryout model, I don't see a lot of these today.[1] With that being said, my wife and I stayed at this church for thirteen years and remain close to its people and leadership to this day. The thoroughness of the process gave us an idea of what each of us was getting into when agreeing to join one another in ministry.

TRUTH: HIRING MATTERS

Note to the Reader: You might be wondering, "Why is there a chapter on hiring a youth minister in a book for youth ministry parents?" It's a good question. This chapter is included for two reasons:

* You may be at a church where the authority to lead the youth ministry is given to an individual parent leader and/or counsel of parents. In that case, you need to know how what to look for in a youth minister.
* You may be at a church where the authority and leadership responsibilities for hiring and firing are given to a senior staff member and/or church leadership counsel. In that case, you need to know the process leaders go through in hiring a youth minister so you can support the hire.

WHY?

Most of you reading this book are parents and leaders in "Western" churches. Therefore, you are familiar with the hiring process in the secular world. A job is posted, calls are made, résumés are received, more calls are made, interviews are scheduled, a decision is made, negotiations over compensation are completed, and a professional agreement for work is reached. There are similarities in the secular and church hiring process. Here are a few unique considerations that matter when hiring a youth minister:

It's more than a job—it's a calling. Those who will apply (or you will ask to apply) see their work as a calling. That is, something the Lord has gifted them and prepared them to do in the service of the church. For some, their calling involves a profound moment (a kind of "Burning Bush" event), when they felt and understood their work in ministry. For others, it involved a series of subtle confirmations from family, friends, and church members, urging them to work with youth. Therefore, it's *personal.*

It's more than a job—you are inviting them into your family. Most likely, if you hire someone to landscape and take care of your yard, you will not invite them into your home for meals, let them take week-long trips with your kids, and open up to them concerning life's most difficult questions. That level of trust is not implied or given to landscaping hires. That level of trust *is* implied and a given for youth ministry hires. Therefore, know this when approaching the hiring process.

Book chapter and verse? It is all over the Bible. The expectation of treatment, authority, and access to the heart given to the prophets and priests of Israel is an example of calling and family. The expectation of treatment, authority, and access to the heart given to the disciples of Christ is an example of calling and family. In both of these examples, sometimes they were treated poorly and even killed by those who did not like or accept this relationship. But this is seen all throughout Scripture.

Read carefully what I am about to say and don't read more into these words than what is intended: *Ministers are hired to work* with *you, not* for *you.* Read those words again if needed. Yes, accountability is found on both sides of the hiring/working relationship, but the hiring of a youth minister (or any minister for that matter) is uniquely different.

Book chapter and verse? Read the letters of Paul. You will see the *with* not *for* relationship (with accountability) in each of these correspondences.

This is why hiring matters so much. You are affirming a person's calling and inviting them into your family. This makes the hiring experience much more than a talent show, popularity contest, or simple transaction for services rendered.

HOW?

There are tremendous resources available for helping churches find, interview, and hire youth ministry candidates. Our favorites are listed at the end of this book. You will be flooded with a lot of great information, so let me offer a few suggestions on how to start the hiring process.

Assemble a Good Team

Similar to the secular hiring process, know who has the actual authority to make the hire and who has the authority to develop and execute the team and process that will bring the name of a finalist to the top for hiring consideration. Yes, this may be the same person or group. Regardless, *clearly* name the hiring leadership group or person and clearly name those responsible for developing and executing the hiring process. The word *clearly* is used intentionally. If either of these leadership positions fails to support the other and respect the process, problems will occur. (The word *will* is also used intentionally.)

Who should be on your hiring team? Those who can clearly articulate the two areas below. Those who represent the various constituencies of your youth ministry. And those who have a current, working understanding of adolescent needs and families (teachers, administrators, coaches, and professional counselors are great additions to hiring committee members). Old youth ministers can be a great asset to a hiring committee. With that said, be careful of the old youth minister who may be stuck in the "back in my day" mindset.

Who should lead your hiring team? The person who has the emotional and spiritual maturity to lead and advocate for committee members. The person who has the ability to embrace, value, and communicate the words of dissenting voices in order to add value to the entire hiring process. The person who is held as a leader by the church and can clearly articulate and execute the process.

Know What You Are Looking for in a Youth Minister

This can be one of the most challenging phases of the hiring process. But with the right leader and team in place (see above), it can also be the most rewarding and save a lot of time.

How do you know what you are looking for in a youth minister? The simple answer is by determining the particular context and needs of your youth ministry. These questions will help you get started:

* How big is your city/town?
* How close are you to other cities/towns?
* How many schools are in your city/town?
* What is the socioeconomic makeup of your church?
* What is the socioeconomic makeup of your city/town?
* What is the average age of your church's congregation?
* What is the average age of your city/town's population?
* How many adults are involved, or seek to be involved, in your ministry? Are they utilized, and do they view their roles as volunteers or chaperones? Why?
* Do you want a married couple? Why or why not?
* Would you work with a single youth minister? Why or why not?

* Do you want someone full time or part time? How will that work?
* Do you want a college graduate? A Bible ministry degree holder? Why or why not?
* Do you want someone with experience? How much? Why?
* Will any of these items be negotiable? Which ones? Why?

How do you reflect what you are looking for in a job description? The simple answer, again, is that after you determine your context and the needs of your youth ministry, this begins to materialize rather quickly. Frequently, Walter and I (David) receive and are asked to evaluate job descriptions. If we know the context and needs of the youth ministry, the feedback process is rather simple. If we do not know the context and needs of the youth ministry, we start with the above questions in order to offer helpful feedback. The goal of a good job description is to present the clearest picture of expectations possible.

Know What Your Nonnegotiable Areas Are

While often stated in a job description, most nonnegotiable items, often by accident, find their way into the interview phase of the hiring process. It is best to know what your nonnegotiable items currently look like before the hiring process starts. Notice I used the words *currently look like*, because "nonnegotiable" can sometimes be "not yet negotiable." It is all right to say "not yet negotiable" to interviewing youth ministers. Here are a few questions to get you started on determining your nonnegotiables in programming and theological comfort. Brace yourself; some of these are dicey:

Programming

* Is there a summer camp your students have to participate in?
* Is there a summer mission trip your students have to participate in?
* Is there a yearly retreat, lock-in, trip, or similar your students have to participate in?
* Is there a church-wide event in which the youth ministry is expected to participate in?
* Is there a certain school the youth ministry has catered to? Are the youth minister's kids expected to attend that school?
* Is there a certain group of people who have served and led in the ministry and are expected to keep volunteering in it? Who are they? Why are they a nonnegotiable presence?
* Are there members of the youth staff who are "untouchable" and outside of your leadership? Why?
* In short, what is considered nonnegotiable about youth ministry programming? Why?

Theological Comfort

* What is your view on the authority, interpretation, and application of Scripture?

    This question is in need of further explanation. We work with hiring committees who are at times frustrated with applicants who, in their opinion, answer this question "incorrectly" when the statements "ability to accurately interpret and apply Scripture" and "believe in the authority of Scripture" are clearly stated on the job description. I don't want to ruin all the fun you will have answering this question with your hiring committee, but what is often sought after in these types of statements is the answer to these questions: "Do you believe what we believe and do church the way we do church?" It is a humbling reality; two people can read the same Scripture and arrive at different conclusions while both hold to the authority of Scripture.

* What are the "acceptable" forms of worship in your church? Are there different forms allowed in youth group? Why or why not?

* Are women fully accepted in leadership roles? Which ones? Why or why not? What about in youth group? Do girls have different limits on leadership than boys? Why or why not?

* What are your church's beliefs and practices concerning the LGBTQ community?

* Is there a certain political party and/or ideology your church aligns itself with?

* What is your church's belief regarding the sacraments, and how are they practiced (Lord's Supper, baptism, etc.)?

* How does your church feel about alcohol, dancing, and so on?

* Does your youth ministry participate in youth programming outside of your denomination?

Identifying nonnegotiable areas will save both the church and prospective hire a lot of time and discomfort.

Pray, Reflect, Listen, Pray . . . Repeat

All throughout the hiring process, do these things. Do these things often and, as mentioned, repeat.

Confidentiality

Especially if the minister you are interviewing is working at another church or organization, keep introductory conversations confidential. If the interview process becomes public and does not work out, the youth minister risks losing his or her credibility and influence at that church. At some point, typically when references are checked, notify the youth pastor candidate that you will be speaking with others about his or her application. A breach of confidentiality can result in a rough transition from and into the ministry.

 ### NOW?

If you are in need of a youth minister, you may have skipped straight to this chapter. That is totally OK and the reason we wrote the book the way we did. You are looking for a youth minister, so what now?

* Acknowledge the differences between hiring an employee and hiring a youth minister. Talk about and explain the reasons for these differences.
* While diving into the hiring guide resources provided at the end of the book, consider beginning your hiring journey by following the suggestions on how to start the hiring process.

Finally, *realize the hiring of a new youth minister is, more than likely, not the answer to your struggling, dying church.* That may have sounded a bit rough, but there is truth in that statement, and it needs to be embraced. I find churches that believe if they find the right youth minister to revitalize their youth programming, then young families will return, and the church will flourish and grow. That mindset is dated. Certainly a strong youth ministry impacts church growth, but today, a strong youth ministry impacts church growth because youth ministry *is* the church's ministry. Youth ministry is not an isolated, compartmentalized "programming piece." Youth ministry is an integrated, intergenerational "programming focus."[2]

"I am sorry; this will never happen again. Can you help me fix this?"

These humble and heartfelt words were offered in the wake of a bad hiring process and subsequent separation from a youth minister. The steps outlined above had been bypassed and the job description had been unclear. As a result, tensions quickly flared, and the new youth minister faced opposition from other staff members and families.

A revamped hiring process and a clear job description allowed a new youth minister to be found—one who quickly thrived in the position.

TRUTH: HIRING MATTERS.

FIRING
MATTERS

How You Leave a Church Is Just as Important as How You Arrive at a Church. Separations Can Be Difficult.

I (David) have done better things.

"We are going to go in a different direction with your position. Your employment with us will end this summer." These are difficult words to hear and difficult to speak. And they should be! Words like this create a wave of reaction and can't be taken back.

Those who love the minister find the firing unjustified.

Those who dislike the minister may think of the firing as late and mismanaged.

Those who are neutral may want to rush into the hiring process.

In the middle of all this emotional chaos swirls the youth minister, his or her advocates, and your decision to terminate employment.

Yep, I have done better things.

Firing people is difficult. Even if it is warranted due to bad performance or behavior, it is still difficult. However, firing is often necessary for both the youth minister and the church to find the best ministry or minister to fit each's context and mission. So how you go about the process of firing is important.

TRUTH: FIRING MATTERS

Note to the Reader: You might be wondering, "Why is there a chapter on firing a youth minister in a book for youth ministry parents?" It's a good question. This chapter is included for two reasons:

* You may be at a church where the authority to lead the youth ministry is given to an individual parent leader and/or counsel of parents. In that case, you need to know how to terminate a youth minister.
* You may be at a church where the authority and leadership responsibilities for hiring and firing are given to a senior staff member and/or church leadership counsel. In that case, you need to know the process leaders go through in terminating a youth minister so you can understand the decision and avoid unnecessary conflict. And if you are currently on the hunt to get your youth minister fired, this chapter will let you know how to evaluate and handle your concerns in a Christ-like, practical manner.

WHY?

It matters how you fire people. It matters to both the youth minister and the church. As mentioned in the chapter on hiring, it's *personal*. Remember, a youth minister's calling and his or her connection with your family will be impacted.

Even though the process is similar to any secular termination, getting fired from a ministry is personal and emotional for both the one being fired and the church doing the firing. If it is not, I (David) believe your hiring process needs renovation. Notice the emotion of the Ephesian elders when Paul speaks his farewell words: "When Paul had finished speaking, he knelt down with all of them and prayed. They all wept as they embraced him and kissed him. What grieved them most was his statement that they would never see his face again" (Acts 20:36–38).

No, Paul was not fired, but the separation caused deep, authentic pain in the leadership. The separation was personal. For whatever the reason of termination, your separation from the youth minister will be personal and emotional for both parties.

The following verses remind us not only how but why we approach the firing of a youth minister with great diligence and care (emphasis mine throughout):

> Those who consider themselves religious and yet do not keep a *tight rein on their tongues deceive themselves,* and their religion is worthless. (James 1:26)

> But David said to Abishai, "Don't destroy him! Who can lay a hand on the LORD's anointed and *be guiltless*?" (1 Sam. 26:9)

> All you need to say is simply 'Yes' or 'No'; *anything beyond this comes from the evil one.* (Matt. 5:37)

> Not many of you should become teachers, my fellow believers, because you know that we who teach *will be judged more strictly.* We all stumble in many

ways. Anyone who is never at fault in what they say is perfect, able to keep their whole body in check . . . All kinds of animals, birds, reptiles and sea creatures are being tamed and have been tamed by mankind, but *no human being can tame the tongue*. It is a restless evil, full of deadly poison . . . Who is wise and understanding among you? Let them show it by their good life, by deeds done in the *humility* that comes from wisdom. *But if you harbor bitter envy and selfish ambition in your hearts, do not boast about it or deny the truth. Such "wisdom" does not come down from heaven but is earthly, unspiritual, demonic. For where you have envy and selfish ambition, there you find disorder and every evil practice. But the wisdom that comes from heaven is first of all pure; then peaceloving, considerate, submissive, full of mercy and good fruit, impartial and sincere.* Peacemakers who sow in peace reap a harvest of righteousness. (James 3:1–2, 7–8, 13–18)

What business is it of mine to judge those outside the church? *Are you not to judge those inside?* God will judge those outside. "Expel the wicked person from among you." (1 Cor. 5:12–13)

Brothers and sisters, if someone is caught in a sin, you who live by the Spirit should restore that person *gently*. But watch yourselves, or you also may be tempted. Carry each other's burdens, and in this way you will fulfill the law of Christ. *If anyone thinks they are something when they are not, they deceive themselves. Each one should test their own actions. Then they can take pride in themselves alone, without com-paring themselves to someone else, for each one should carry their own load.* (Gal. 6:1–5)

They [Paul and Barnabas] had such a sharp disagree-ment that *they parted company.* (Acts 15:39)

You may be wondering why I listed all these scriptures rather than simply referencing them. Well, if you are like me, you might have a bad habit of skipping references in order to get to the author's words. We dare not skip this when addressing the firing of a youth minister. The counsel of Scripture is impera-tive to determining why and how we terminate that relationship.

There are many other beneficial scriptures to consider in the firing process. These were chosen because of personal preference. Furthermore, all these verses have a rich and necessary context to consider. What can be gathered from the given highlights is this:

* The firing process should not be taken lightly.
* The reason for the firing (and motivation) should be clear and, as far as humanly possible, above reproach.
* The power and impact of one's words throughout the process should be governed.
* Moral failure as well as the inability to work together can be causation for a firing.

Simply put, approach the firing of a youth minister with theo-logical reflection and clearly justified and articulated causation. No matter what, the separation will be personal. Don't make it worse by forgoing theological reflection and preparation.

HOW?

I am hoping you read the *why* before skipping ahead to the *how*. If not, go back and read that section first (I will wait). OK, now that you have theologically reflected and prepared, which I realize is not that easy, let me present a few suggestions when firing a youth minister.

Gather Information

If you are considering firing a youth minister, you already know information is often easy to come by. People, especially the disgruntled, love to talk. People, especially those damaged by a minister's moral failure, need to feel safe bringing their concerns to church leadership. Even so, this is where theological reflection is of great importance, because leaders must discern what is *worthy* (sorry to use that word) and cause for termination.

Some people will always remain disgruntled and never be satisfied with the youth ministry, so leaders have to be discerning. Regardless, it is best practice to let the youth minister know of such talk so they will be aware of the "disgruntled" and better navigate the situation. Trust me, if there is a problem with the youth minister, leaders will hear from people. Don't shield the youth minister from that; bring them into the conversation, be open about the concerns, and document the meetings.

In the case of moral failure, listen and document the information you are receiving carefully. Be sure to let the one giving you the information know that as a leader, you will have to act and do what's best with the information they are sharing. As they share, do not justify, defend, and/or give explanation to what you are hearing reported about the youth minister's conduct. Again, listen and document:

* If it is a matter that must involve Child Protective Services, follow the protocol given on your state's website. If you are a parent receiving this information from your or another student, share your documented conversation with the youth minister's direct supervisor as soon as possible. Even though it may be tempting to look for support elsewhere, avoid sharing the information with others.

* If it is another moral failure, listen and document. Again, avoid sharing the information with others and talk with the youth minister's direct supervisor.

Remember these things:

* If the information is coming from someone who does not want to be identified or an anonymous source, be careful and hold tightly to the information.

* Never use words such as *many families* or *several people* unless you are willing to share those names with your youth minister.

* It is my (David's) opinion that the "information gathering" process be communicated with the youth minister as clearly and prudently as possible.

Consult Policy, Procedure, and Documentation

This will vary with the structure of each church, but most have written policy, procedure, and documentation to follow for hiring and firing ministers. If not, it would be wise to consult a nearby church that has written this out in order to assure your firing process is above reproach. In short, while some states (or countries) allow the termination of employees at will, given the personal nature of firing a minister, it is best practice to cite documented meetings / performance reviews that validate performance and/or moral failures that are unresolved or call for justified termination. All termination correspondence should be documented and provided to the youth minister in writing.

Be Clear and Articulate

The decision has been made and it is time to let the youth minister know he or she is being terminated. Be clear and articulate about the reasons for the firing. A youth minister may know the news is coming; many do. If not, they will ask questions as to why they are being let go. If you have ever been fired, you know a person's thinking may go numb and/or operate slowly when hearing tough news. Clarity is key. On a related note, be certain that you articulate the reason termination is occurring with the church body. Yes, there are things that need to be confidential and are unable to be shared, but a lack of clear communication from leadership after a firing produces a climate of distrust among congregants.

Provide Beneficial Severance

Many churches have written policies concerning severance packages. If your church does not, consider reaching out to a church that does for counsel. In short, whether the termination was based on failure or fit, give the youth minister a beneficial severance. He or she will need time to process the firing. Again, we are dealing with the firing of a youth minister; it is personal. Also, it can take a while for a youth minister to find another church to serve. Most of the churches I have worked with offer *a minimum* of three months' severance for the terminated minister.

Provide a Reference

An offer to provide a solid reference can be a gift to the youth minister, though this may not be a thing to mention when communicating the decision to fire him or her. If the reason for termination makes a solid reference impossible to give, let the youth minister know that he or she should not list you as a reference for future church employment. In that case, the information *should* be shared at the moment of termination.[1]

Be Compassionate and Empathic

The above steps can be conducted with business-like precision and little emotion. However, even in the worst of scenarios, can I encourage you to demonstrate great compassion and empathy to the youth minister being fired? It is of great benefit, no matter the circumstance of termination, to offer payment for the youth minister to have several sessions with a licensed mentor, coach, or counseling professional.

If I may be so bold, I have two items that need to be reconsidered, and perhaps repented, regarding how we fire youth ministers. One, I know there are occasions when a gag order attached to severance pay is appropriate but *not* at the alarming level seen in today's US churches. Again, if there is nothing to hide, why is the condition placed? If the fired minister begins to create division in his or her departure from the church, then handle the situation at that point. Starting off with a gag order breeds unhealthy questions and assumptions for both the minister and leadership. Two, requesting a youth minister read a prepared, generalized statement that does not reflect the true reason for their firing is dishonest and will breed unhealthy questions and assumptions in both the minister and leadership as well. Statements like "I have decided to resign in order to pursue other opportunities" when there's not another opportunity are disingenuous.

Walter and I both already know and understand the push-back many leaders will have regarding these two items. We also understand that discernment is key, and often difficult to determine, when firing a youth minister. Still, if at all possible, we have to stop the blanket gag orders and generic, prepared statements, using these as a last resort when terminating a youth minister.

 ## NOW?

Unless it is a moral failure that demands immediate action, if you are on the verge of terminating your youth minister, I suggest you do the following:

* Prayerfully and slowly go back and read the Scripture listed in the "Why?" section. Is there something that grabs your attention? Why?
* Check to be sure that you are able to carry out all of the above steps of termination with clear motivation and due process.
* Pray. Pray for the one being terminated, your leadership, and the future of both the church and the youth minister being fired.

The conversation was difficult and painful, feelings were hurt; it was *personal*. However, the reasons for termination and the process forward were made as clear as possible.

The result? A better fit was found for the youth ministry, and the terminated youth minister was affirmed and supported in the start of a new ministry. A ministry that continues to impact hundreds of teenagers a year to this day.

TRUTH: FIRING MATTERS.

MONEY MATTERS

Money Is Not Everything.
But It Is Still Important.

"I don't know."

That was my answer to my wife after my second trip to an interview with a church. She was asking about the salary range. I (Walter) had spent over forty-eight hours over about four weeks with this church, talking to dozens of staff, elders, and parents. And had no idea what this church was able to offer.

Was it going to be poverty wages?

Were we going to be able to consider buying a home in the area?

Would I be able to continue my graduate studies in theology?

All of these were vital issues that needed to be considered, and I had nothing to give to my wife. As the candidate, I did not know if this was information that I was supposed to ask for. Shouldn't it have been provided to me?

TRUTH: MONEY MATTERS

WHY?

We have both consulted with dozens and dozens of churches with regards to finding and hiring a youth minister. Perhaps the question we get asked the most is, "How much would be a fair salary?" While that is an important question that we will get to, what we also observe is that more times than not, the topic of compensation is the one that is most avoided during the process. Search teams will talk about theology, their stance on various worship practices, the role of women in public leadership, the importance of camp, and so on without ever approaching the topic of salary and compensation.

The result? Well-meaning churches invest a tremendous amount of time, effort, and energy in the search process only to come up empty because the compensation package is a deal breaker. One of the churches that I interviewed with brought me out for visits twice and then brought my whole family out twice (that's four visits) before they ever broached the topic of the salary. This caused tremendous consternation and anxiety for me and my family. While we loved what this church was about and felt it would be a great fit, we were worried that we would not be able to live, much less thrive, on what they would be able to offer us in the way of a salary. Don't get us wrong; people do not go into youth ministry to become the next Bill Gates or Elon Musk, but they do want to put a roof over their heads and food in their bellies.

The Bible is clear that finances are an important topic. It is discussed in Scripture more than almost any other topic. We read that the "love of money is the root of all evil" (1 Tim. 6:10 KJV) and the "no one can serve two masters" (Matt. 6:24). If one's motivation for doing youth ministry is financial, we would have very different concerns for such a candidate. However, we have watched dozens of wonderful men and women who were extremely gifted and passionate about ministry depart their calling in order to survive because they were living at or below the poverty line. While we are not advocating that congregations supply their youth ministers with a private jet and a security detail to protect their gold bling, we are asking churches to invest in those who are doing such important work.

For years, the legend has been that the average tenure of a youth minister hovered at about eighteen months to two years.[1] Sadly, many times the deciding factor for such short stints was a financial one. Thankfully, in recent decades, the longevity of such positions is on the rise. We have also seen many more career youth pastors than in years past as churches have invested necessary resources to keep their youth ministers on staff longer. Longer ministry means deeper ministry. Longer ministry tenures also have a deeper impact on adolescents, as they do not have to face the revolving door of incoming and outgoing youth ministers and the lack of trust and broken relationships that come with it. As we will discuss later, we recognize that not all churches can compensate for longevity, but they should at least consider it.

Since many youth ministry search teams are composed of volunteers as opposed to a human resources department, chances are that many on the search team are parents like you who have little to no hiring experience. Furthermore, determining who is responsible for making and communicating the offer is assumed or left for the elders at the very end. So how then does a mom or dad like you approach such a topic?

HOW?

In our experience, there are a number of different philosophies that guide a church's compensation policy. Oftentimes, these policies remain in place through generations because "this is the way it's always been done" and leadership has not taken the time to stop and consider the effect of their philosophy on staffing and longevity in ministry. Here are a few common philosophies that dictate compensation practices:

> *Youth ministers take a vow of poverty.* Sadly, many churches have adopted the philosophy that a call to youth ministry requires a vow of poverty. Not only is this tremendously discouraging to well-equipped men and women who want to minister to teens; it is not the role of the church to impose a vow of poverty. That is a vow one voluntarily submits to.

> *It's an entry-level position.* The reality is that most churches are small churches of about 150.[2] The next ministry hire after a preacher is generally a youth minister. As a result, budgets are generally small and have to be stretched to be able to make the hire in the first place. Some churches are tremendously apologetic about not being able to pay as much as they would like to. We advise churches in these situations not to be apologetic, just honest about the fact that they cannot pay as much as they would like. However, we also advise that these churches lean into this, take on a Kingdom perspective, and promote their position as an entry-level ministry position. Present your position as a three-to-four-year position. During that time, resource the ministers with opportunities for continuing education at conferences or seminary, help

building their ministry library, and mentoring from your senior minister/pastor. Give them the grace and freedom to make mistakes and learn the ropes of ministry. And when they have outgrown your church financially, send them with love into the Kingdom to do more ministry somewhere else.

Compensation is based on experience or position. We know of a lot of churches who pay their preacher double what the youth minister makes. Such a metric inadvertently values the role of the preacher as twice as important as the youth minister.

Consider developing a compensation package that takes into account a minister's education and experience. I was at a church that compensated based on our experience and education. So I knew that after I had put in the time and work that my preacher had, I too would be compensated similarly. (I never knew what my colleagues got paid but that this was how our financial policy was developed.) As a result, there existed mutual admiration and respect between us and our ministries. There was not the resentment that comes from feeling undervalued, as I had felt at other churches where the policy was to pay me less because of my position. Compensating for experience treats a candidate with respect and communicates that their ministry is just as important as the others in the church.

Compensation encourages longevity. Some churches build certain incentives to help ministers stay longer. Benefits like sabbaticals after a certain amount of time served, increasing paid time off (PTO) every year, and increasing salaries after benchmark years (like five or ten years) are just a few ways to incentivize a minister's longevity.

NOW?

Here's how to go about this:

How Much?

So the big question we know you probably have been waiting for is, How much? A good rule of thumb to work with in determining a competitive salary is to look up your local school district's salary schedule for a high school teacher. Many are available online and contain a range that takes into account years of service, education, and experience.[3] I generally tell churches to take that amount and add 10–20 percent, as teachers are not required to work during the summers the way youth ministers are. This will get your church to a competitive salary range for quality candidates.

Timing

When do we talk about money? Many times, the search team does not know the salary range due to the fact that this information and decision are left up to the elders. This also means that most of the people your candidates are communicating with are left without this critical piece of information. This information is vital to their discernment process; they need to know if they will be able to provide adequately for their families. It is tremendously frustrating to not know at least a general ballpark of what that salary and benefits might be. Remember that quality candidates may be considering several ministry options when they are interviewing with your church.

Salary and benefits are also a tremendously delicate topic for candidates to bring up. If they bring it up too early in the process, they risk looking like they are only interested in the money. If they bring it up too late, they (and your church) may have invested far too much time before discovering the ballpark is not adequate for their family's needs. The sooner you can give a candidate this information, the better—for both sides. *It is the responsibility of the search team to offer this information and not the candidate's job to ask for it.*

Get It on Paper

At the end of this document is a sample policy manual as well as a sample offer letter that can help you put down on paper the different benefits and compensation expectations that are being offered. There are countless stories of misunderstandings that have occurred at this part of the process, where the offer is one thing and the candidate thinks it is another, and they start their ministry off on a bad note because they feel cheated. Writing out the offer on paper can avoid any misunderstandings and ensure that everyone is on the same page. Your offer should contain the basics:

> *Salary.* The net pay and the frequency with which the minister will be paid (weekly, biweekly, monthly)

> *Vacation time.* How much time they can take off and when (some ministries factor in all ministry experience in their vacation structure)

> *Medical, dental, vision insurance.* What is covered, and whether it will cover just the candidates or their families as well

Matching retirement plan. What percentage of the salary the church will match for a 401(k)/403(b) plan

It might also include the following:

Compensatory time policy. Some churches have a compensatory time policy for when ministers miss a day off for events like camp or mission trips.

Number of Sundays off per year. Some churches give their ministers one to two Sundays off annually, allowing them time to visit neighboring churches or attend a different church without the pressing expectations of their own work (not only can this prove to be a great way for them to be refreshed spiritually, but they will inevitably gain a new perspective [research] on how to do something that your ministry will benefit from).

Sabbatical policy. Some churches, acknowledging that the creative process of ministry is draining, offer a paid sabbatical policy that allows for extended time away to pursue a variety of other activities to refuel (e.g., study time away, school, creative projects, writing, Sabbath, etc.; some also include a stipend to help with travel and other expenses).

Personal library budget. Some churches offer ministers a personal library fund that allows for ministers to continue learning in order to stay up to date on the scholarship in their areas of ministry.

Continuing education budget. Some churches offer a budget for ministers to attend conferences or to pursue higher education (this benefits your church by equipping them with more skills and knowledge that allows them to do their job more proficiently).

Moving expenses. Some churches offer ministers a budget to cover moving expenses (movers, truck rentals, hotels, food, etc.) to help them transition to their new city.

Back to my (Walter's) interview experience.

Honestly, I was nervous at first. But I needed to give my wife something more concrete than an "I don't know."

I had concerns. If I asked financial compensation questions, would that send a message that all I was concerned about was the money? I also knew that talk of money could make people uncomfortable. And in some parts of the country, financial discussions are considered impolite.

Still, it was a conversation that had to happen!

Thankfully, in the end, the church was exceedingly generous with its offer.

TRUTH: MONEY MATTERS

SABBATH MATTERS

**On the Seventh Day, God Rested.
So Should Your Minister.**

At one of the camps I (Walter) helped lead, all the youth ministers who were part of the leadership team would gather in the Snack Shack to go over the day's events and plan for the next one. Inevitably, we would end up talking for an extra hour or two on a myriad of other "ministry" things. One night, someone made the comment, "Yeah, I am going to have to be in the office first thing on Monday."

"What?!" we all replied.

"Yeah, we have to be in the office every Monday morning."

This was in the midst of about fifteen straight days of camp. We had spent two days in prep with staff, one week with the middle school campers, and one week with the high school campers. All back-to-back. And this youth minister would get back late on Saturday, and then be in church the next day, and then be expected to be in the office, working, on Monday.

TRUTH: SABBATH MATTERS

WHY?

I find it very interesting that God knew that humanity would have to be commanded to practice Sabbath in the Ten Commandments. *Commanded.* We have something dysfunctional in our post-Eden natures that drives us to just work, work, work, work.

In creation, God set up this rhythm of life: work, work, work, work, work, work, *rest*.

This is how we can flourish in life.

It is through Sabbath that we are able to be re-created. Sabbath is our reconnection to the Spirit of God within us. Sabbath reminds us that we are not God and that God is in control. Sabbath reconnects us to our creative natures, which we share with the God revealed in Genesis 1 and 2.

The same is true for your youth minister. While many of us work in cultures that demand eighty-hour weeks and fifteen days of straight work, this is not the way we flourish in the Kingdom. One author puts it this way: Sabbath is "time for being in the midst of a life of doing."[1] What is most interesting in the Ten Commandments is that not only is Sabbath for the people of Israel, whom God gives it to, but it is for their sons, daughters, manservants, maidservants, animals, and aliens within their gates. In other words, *everyone* is to benefit from Sabbath, whether or not they believe in God. James Bryan Smith observes rightfully, "The number one enemy of Christian spiritual formation today is exhaustion."[2] One of the most-cited reasons for men and women leaving the ministry is not financial but due to burnout.

Barbara Brown Taylor notes this: "God worked hard for six days and then God rested, performing the consummate act of divine freedom by doing nothing at all. Furthermore, the rest was so delicious that God did not call it good, or even very good. Instead, God blessed the seventh day and called it holy, making Sabbath the first sacred thing in all creation."[3]

This is how serious God is about this idea of Sabbath rest.

HOW?

If your church has not already helped encourage/demand that your youth minister observe Sabbath, there are a couple of policies that you can encourage your leadership to implement.

Sabbath Day

Insist that your youth minister designate a specific day of the week to take his or her Sabbath, preferably during the week. Why? Sundays are just not a day off for a minister. And many times, a youth ministry event falls on a Saturday, which can easily get in the way of a Sabbath. I personally took Fridays as my Sabbath. When I took Mondays as Sabbath, I personally felt I was starting the week a day short. If a youth ministry event like a youth retreat dictated that I leave on a Friday, then I took Thursday as Sabbath.

This concept needs to be enforced at a leadership level with accountability. On Fridays that I would "pop in" to the office, I would get a gentle ribbing from my colleagues telling me to leave and go home. Sometimes this was in jest. But it was often also out of concern that I not burn myself out.

Compensatory Time

If there are events like camps or mission trips where a youth pastor must miss their Sabbath day, then have a policy that they are to take it sometime in the next seven days after such an event.

Some churches have a policy that you can "bank" time, which has good intentions. However, for many, what happens is that the banked days are never used.

Vacation Time

Insist, insist, *insist* that your youth pastor takes their vacation (PTO) days every year. I was working at a church that let me "bank" my PTO. After several years, I had over twelve weeks of unused PTO. While this can be considered noble, our elders then began to institute a "use it or lose it" policy for unused PTO. This was not a punishment but a loving nudge to make us take our PTO in order to keep us fresh.

After this policy was enacted, I took my first two-week vacation. It was transformative. You see, in previous years, I would take a week of vacation. What would happen is that we would leave after church on Sunday, I would enjoy Monday and Tuesday, but by Wednesday, my mind would inevitably drift to the coming weekend and Sunday's responsibility. Mentally, I was taken away from wherever we had traveled to for rest.

When I was away for two weeks, when that first Wednesday rolled around, I knew I had another nine days until I had responsibilities. That was an eternity mentally, physically, and spiritually. That vacation, it felt like I was gone for a month. It was so refreshing and renewing. When I came back, I was a new minister.

Sabbatical

Ministry is a taxing vocation for one's soul, body, family, and spirit. It requires a tremendous amount of creativity to develop and teach different topics and subjects year after year. Creativity is also required for thinking of and developing different retreat and camp themes. Summers are long and arduous with endless arrays of activities, events, and trips. This is not meant to be a laundry list of complaints. This is an observation. Many churches have begun to recognize this and develop a sabbatical policy to give their ministers a season to be renewed. To learn more about sabbaticals, see "A Word on Sabbaticals" at the end of this book.

 NOW?

You may be reading this section thinking to yourself, "Why is this in here? I am a parent. Isn't this a church leadership thing?" And you may be right. However, sometimes these kinds of policies happen because of the advocacy work of volunteers and concerned parents like you:

> *Ask around.* You might begin by doing an informal survey of the different policies your church has in place for PTO, vacation time, and compensatory time. You may find that there are some loosely understood policies but nothing in writing. Many times, policies that are loosely understood fail to serve those they are designed for. An "understood" policy puts the minister in a difficult position regarding whether they actually are able to take advantage of said policies. Your questions may be the impetus leadership needs to develop formal policies.

> *Kindly suggest.* If your questions determine that no policies exist or that your policies are inadequate, then volunteer to write some for leadership to consider. Remember, many leadership roles that possess such decision-making power are filled with well-intentioned

and underresourced volunteers. Taking the burden of researching and writing from a church leader's plate, from someone who also has a full-time job and a family, may be enthusiastically welcomed. It will at least light a fire under the leadership.

I wish the story I started this chapter with had a good ending. It didn't. The youth minister was out of ministry in less than twelve months after those comments.

Understandably, he burnt out.

TRUTH: SABBATH MATTERS

CONCLUSION

Where Do You Go from Here?

We have offered dozens of things you can do to support your youth minister and youth ministry. Depending on your personality, this can be a good or bad thing. It is a good thing if you come away with a macrolevel view of your role in your church's youth ministry. It is a good thing if you can pick up one or two things to do now or do differently. Excellent. That is one of our visions for this book.

But . . .

If you are the type of person who has a list of twenty-three different things to jump into and start doing, we respectfully ask you to step back from this ledge and take a breath. If you heard over and over, "You should do this" and "You should do that," while you read our book, that was never our intention. Historically, churches have been good at should-ing all over people. No one wants to be should-ed on. We hope this was not your experience.

Here are a few next steps you might consider:

Conclusion

Some of you need to do less. Your family calendar looks like a logistic plan for Amazon Prime delivery for the upper Midwest region. The last thing your family calendar needs is one more thing. Hopefully, you can take what you've read here and put it on a shelf for a simpler time in the rhythm of life.

Some of you need to do nothing. Hopefully this book was an affirmation that you are doing a good job. Perhaps you even saw yourself in some of our stories or could contribute your own ideas for a second edition of this book after it sells a hundred thousand copies. If so, we want to say, "Thank you for your ministry to teens!"

Some of you need to just do one thing. Hopefully as you read, one thing that continued to come to mind was, "I could do that." If we did a good job with this book, that idea came up more than once. We ask that you only pick one of the ideas and run with it. Then pick up another. And then . . . you get the idea. Your youth minister will be thankful for your partnership in ministry.

To all of you . . . thank you. We know how busy life can be. To pick up a book titled *Practical Wisdom for Youth Group Parents* means you care at a level that matters and can make a real difference in the church. Youth ministry depends on people like you. People willing to devote the time and effort to read something like this and put it into action.

A WORD ON SABBATICALS

Contrary to what many think, sabbaticals are not vacations. They are designed to give your minister a break from the normal routine and responsibilities of ministry—but often in order to give them new ideas and perspectives *on ministry.*

> *Purpose.* Generally, a sabbatical is designed to help your minister think about his or her work at your church from a different perspective. This can be done in a variety of ways; here are a few examples of ways people have used their sabbatical to enhance their ministries in their local churches:
>
> > *A "tour" of youth ministries.* Traveling to a variety of different youth ministries in the region to see how others do ministry. Included in this would be some shadow time with the youth pastors in those churches. One can harvest a multitude of ideas through such an experience.
> >
> > *A silent retreat.* Spending a weekend or even a week at a local seminary or retreat center to pray, reflect, and vision cast. Many Christian camps and

retreat centers have such services available to full-time pastors. Some even have spiritual directors onsite to help guide this time in silence.

Continuing education. Taking theology courses. Many seminaries and graduate programs have short courses in summer and winter semesters that ministers can take to enhance their understanding of the Bible, ministry, and spiritual development.

Conferences. Joining conferences they might not normally be able to. While many churches plan for their ministers to attend a youth ministry conference annually, a sabbatical gives them an opportunity to do more. They may attend an "out of the box" conference they would not have considered in the past and shore up a specific area of their ministry: perhaps something in management, homiletics, spiritual direction, or creativity.

Reading. Developing a list of books that you have always wanted to read and taking the time to read them. This could include getting away to a place for a few weeks that is off the grid, without internet or television to distract you, and reading.

Length. Many sabbatical policies are designed to encourage ministry staff toward longevity. For example, we have seen churches give one week of sabbatical every three years, four weeks in one's fifth year, or eight weeks in one's seventh year.

Compensation. Sabbatical policies generally continue to compensate ministers with their regular salaries and benefits. The sabbatical time does not count against their paid time off (PTO). Some policies do allow for PTO to be taken to extend the sabbatical a bit longer.

Funding. Many programs also have a budget for travel, lodging, and other expenses to help fund the objectives of the sabbatical. A helpful rule of thumb might be $1,000 for every week of sabbatical, maxing out at $5,000.

IN THEIR OWN WORDS

Toward the end of this project, we were interested in whether we had gone over all that needed to be covered in this book. So we asked our friends on Facebook:

> Youth ministry friends, we're finishing up a book for youth ministry parents. What are a few things you would like parents to know (or do) that would help support you and assist in building a thriving youth ministry?

Two things happened. One, we received affirmation that the information covered was sufficient to publish. And second, our peers (and a few parents and volunteer leaders who chimed in as well) had a lot of great, and often cathartic, things to say on the topic of parents and youth ministry. The responses were a blessing to our writing. So we decided to share the blessing, and challenge, of their responses, *in their own words*:

> Volunteers are always needed for *all* kinds of things, *and your kids love for you to be involved*!

Support, not surveillance. They should look at us as partners and not watch us to see what we do wrong. Partner with us when we plan, prepare, and play.

Our role as youth ministers is not to take them as sixth or seventh graders and download Jesus into them. Our role is to support what you're doing and teaching at home. Please don't expect us to fix your students and make them Christian by the time they graduate. That process started the day you brought them into the world. We want to equip you to be your children's youth ministers at home. We need you to read the Bible with your kids. Pray with them at mealtimes—but at other times too. Normalize this discipline. Talk to your kids about Jesus. Make it normal and natural.

Essentially, monkey see, monkey do. If they want their students to be disciples, and live out their faith, the parents must lead by example.

If you have a problem with the youth minister, don't talk to the preacher, the elders, the deacons, the other parents, the other students, and your friends first. Talk to the youth minister.

Their teen having friends here isn't the goal . . . (sidenote: though it will be a by-product!). I know that may sound bad at first, but there is tons of context. Too many times, I've seen parents come to / leave a church based on if their kid had a close friend in the group. Mostly it involved church hopping so I'm not saying they quit their faith, but it just teaches other unfortunate things when you show that is how to respond. A few times, a few families even went back and forth between two churches based on which of their kids were currently in the group and who they best fit with. Other things, like countless "Who else is going on that trip?" or "They only want to go if _____ is" dilutes the message being the most important thing. I'm all up for fellowship and friend-ship as it is needed in the church, but I've seen lately how that is the goal of more and more parents today. Probably more of an issue in metro areas and the Bible Belt than what others may encounter though.

I agree with the idea of not church hopping, but one of my regrets is not leaving a church when I knew, from the time my son was in seventh or eighth grade, it was not a good fit. I loved the congregation that we had attended since he was a baby, so I kept hoping and kept active, but when a child goes from a small class (fifth and sixth) to a youth group that has hundreds of kids . . . that is not a fit for everyone. And yes, this was a large metroplex church. I think the smaller youth groups that I grew up in allow for more connections with positive role models. So I guess my advice is, know your kid, and don't stay just because *you* feel comfortable. Find a place where your child can grow and have other adults walking alongside you, helping grow their faith.

Be available; sit on the porch and be available. God will open the doors at the right time, then walk in faith. Be authentic; kids can see through you. Yes it's scary, and it's OK to not have all the answers; that's God's job.

As a former youth minister and parent of teens . . . have the hard conversations. Share failures, faith challenges, ask about what they're feeling and experiencing, and share your own need for grace. Also, find ways to grow in your own relationship with God. Don't expect your kids to have something you don't.

Grounding your kids from youth ministry events and not sports practice/games sends a message.

The goal of our youth ministry is to help your teen build a relationship with God and his Family that will impact their life for eternity. It is not just another group for your teen to hang out with occasionally when there aren't other events going on.

It is often up to parents to take the initiative to get to know the youth minister or even the other families in the ministry that will help create the network they need to be a successful community.

Optimal learning needs mild discord and discomfort, and we are not making it comfortable in order to teach, not because we don't like their child.

Youth ministers are human. Part of being human is our own brokenness and need for forgiveness, grace, and mercy. Understanding your own brokenness as a parent may help you realize that dealing with the minister with grace first instead of accusations may really help any tense situation. Most people get into ministry because they love God, have heard a call, love others, and are doing something that does not have a playbook.

A firm identity in Christ starts at home. We (youth pastors) will affirm and equip students to live into that and certainly share the gospel, but parents/ family can and should play one of the most vital roles in their children's faith development.

The core relationship with Jesus should be modeled at home. Youth ministry enhances the experience, giving many opportunities for that relationship to grow. There are times when a relationship will grow strong out of a youth ministry environment—but that is rare unless some adult is willing to spend many hours of time with the student in a variety of circumstances.

As a former youth minister, the big thing that stands out to me is a lack of boundaries in terms of what a youth minister can/should do. Youth ministers aren't therapists, guidance counselors, or substitute parents, but they can often be put into gray areas, where they are asked to work outside of their competency in these areas. Some of my worst seasons of minis- try were working with kids who had mental health issues but their parents refused to send them to ther- apy because they "just needed Jesus." Professional/ ethical boundaries are definitely something that parents would benefit from knowing about.

I think one thing could be helping parents recognize that their child's relationship with Christ is more important than their grades at school or how many extracurricular activities they're involved in. A lot of kids simply don't have time in their schedule for anything other than that, and a portion of that is due to the pressure put on them to succeed in those areas via themselves, society, parent expectations, etc. I was at my high school until midnight some nights working on projects, and I always put everything I did with school first. Church was a fun thing I did when my schedule allowed it. It's extremely difficult to find a balance with everything, but their relationships with Christ shouldn't be at the bottom of the priority list.

Ownership of the ministry, not just attendance, will keep them rooted and growing.

1. Be an owner in the student ministry, even if that means from afar.

2. Remember that your student and others are not the future but they are the now, able to serve and be an extension of Christ now.

3. Don't talk bad about the student ministry . . . why would your kids ever want to go when you put down the team trying to serve your student? Your voice matters.

Allow the student to understand their own view on faith and not just the traditions of the church and the family.

Know that when a youth volunteer or staff member stays in contact after graduation, their credibility and influence with that student rise considerably.

Youth ministry should be able to be about disciple-ship. It's training and equipping. Your kid doesn't get to skip math class because it wasn't enough fun. If you model church as optional, so will your kids.

The student ministry events need to be treated with at least as much importance as sports, music, hunting trips, etc. If parents don't see church as a priority, no wonder their children don't see church as a priority.

Youth ministry is not the place you send your kids to learn about Jesus. That responsibility falls squarely on you, the parent, because you chose to have chil-dren. Youth ministries should be a support system, a place where spiritual formation can be lived out in a safe space, and a place where consistent participa-tion should be expected. Youth ministries should come alongside you as parents, and help guide you in healthy ways to disciple your children. The youth minister is not responsible for the spiritual formation of your child. Yes, they should assist and be a major part of that support system, but not ultimately the one responsible. Oh, and getting them involved in the life of the church is key to a thriving faith. Help-ing them find and utilize their spiritual gift often while they are young will help them be confident that they have a place in the church when they leave their parent's home. It's not a fail-safe, but it will make a difference.

Now that I'm a shepherd, I get a view that's much different when I was just a parent and a youth and family minister. Parents tend to suggest activities that will suit their teen. I believe the youth minister needs a giant tool bag like Felix the Cat. I've watched successful youth ministers that use many ways to bind the group together. We still need to find a way to reach their hearts so they have a heart for Scripture, each other, and the body of Christ. I attend a youth event every November, and I see the fruit of youth workers who put Christ first. I'm proud of them and the work they do. Some call it "old school"; I believe they demonstrate that it is effective in youth ministry. That's my two (maybe three) cents.

Be transparent and authentic Christian role models. Our kids are surrounded by peers and adults who only "love" them for what they can get from them. Love them for who they are now; even look past current bad decisions. Mistakes made at fifteen, sixteen, seventeen, and eighteen do not define you; be an *adult* and help lead them through tough times.

Offer advice on older men and women getting involved with the youth and their families. For example,

Marriage mentoring

Volunteering at youth events

Planned older/younger events (letting the younger teach the older technology and social media; older teach cooking, sewing, and changing oil, batteries, and tires)

Removing the taboo of therapy is a *huge* problem
for youth to overcome. Families need to encourage
finding a way for kids to get professional help, have
uninterrupted meditation, and connect their spirituality to their physical, emotional, and mental health.

Well, this cuts deep. The way it should.

I don't have kids in a youth group . . . yet. My
oldest is about a year and a half away. So I read your
posts to see what to expect.

I make a point to tell my kids' teachers to contact
me if they need help, volunteers, supplies, etc.

I need to talk to our children's minister. Give
them the same support.

On top of that, our youth minister did something
this week that made my blood boil. Guess I needed to
be reminded that he's human too.

Thanks for sharing, all.

As a parent, not a minister . . . talk to me. And I will
talk to you. These are my babies.

Without an open, honest, truly honest line of
communication, we will all fail,

We all have to stop.

Breathe.

And understand.

Then set a goal to work towards together . . .

The *together* is where we need to focus.

Understanding the role of youth minister/ministry
and the role of parenthood. How they're different and
how they can collaborate but not replace one another.

Church gossip does more damage than Twitter comments.

Parents are quicker to blame youth ministers for something that isn't their fault than the current president is to blame someone else for his own shortcomings.

The high school youth minister cannot in one semester of Sunday school solve a parent's lifetime of psychological child abuse.

The internet has fundamentally changed everything. Do not, do not, *do not* expect the youth minister to engage in apologetics. Apologetics is dead. The internet (and all of the evidence, or lack thereof, and the arguments explaining the problems with outdated apologetic arguments) killed apologetics.

Don't ask the youth minister to do what you aren't willing to do. *You* talk to your kids about sex. Don't foist your responsibility on the youth minister and then blame him or her when you don't like what he or she says.

Pay your youth ministers a living wage. If you pay them like adjuncts, they'll work like adjuncts. Demand that your youth ministers actually learn the Bible, speak intelligently about church history, and engage with the kids who need them the most instead of just growing a beard, doing shirtless CrossFit, taking the cool kids on some Instagram trip to some hipster destination, and calling it "youth ministry."

For my part, I would add that youth ministers are generally younger adults and thus are going to make mistakes out of sheer lack of life experience and that instead of complaining about them or busting them for it, try being a friend giving them the respect of talking to them so they can learn and grow. I think I was twenty-four when I started my first job, and I was coming from an extremely conservative background to one of the more liberal in my fellowship (which still isn't saying much, but that's not what you are asking about right now). Suffice to say that as progressive as I thought I was, I had a lot of things that I needed to grow out of in my theology. When I chose certain curriculums to teach, there were a few parents who rightly questioned the doctrine contained in them, but they complained to everyone who *wasn't me.* I wish so badly that those parents had come to me to express their concerns. I was less than eight years older than many of their kids; I had things to learn, and they *could* have brought me along on my journey out of fundamentalism a bit more quickly. Instead, since they were college professors, they b*&% to their college students about how backwards I was to be teaching that BS. And it was BS, but if they had come to me in the right spirit, like we were on the same team, we all would have been better off. Their kids would have benefited from better teaching. I would have benefited from knowing that I could trust those families to speak to me honestly even if we didn't agree. I've got to think that those parents would have benefited from not being backbiting gossips. Everybody wins. I have more, but that's enough for now. I'll probably have stress dreams tonight from reliving all that as it is.

Reply to emails, texts, and Facebook posts.

Volunteer to chaperone. Their kids are wrong—they (probably) won't ruin everything. Youth pastors aren't perfect. Give them the benefit of the doubt before giving them your complaints. Complaints from parents can cripple a thriving youth ministry.

When I was in ministry, I remember wishing my parents knew that I wanted to partner with them in leading their children to Jesus, not be fully in charge of that. Parents have such a crucial role in their children's lives. Youth pastors only get them for so long each week. It truly is a partnership! Not a drop-off service.

1. Treat your youth minister/pastor as a valuable *supplemental* layer of support and ministry. They aren't there to parent your child. They are there to support you as a parent.

2. Show up *on time* to pick up your kid. Your youth pastor has given up their own family time in order to take your kid on an epic adventure—showing up late afterward is disrespectful and tells them that your time is more valuable than theirs.

3. If you have a complaint—go to them directly *and* in kindness. Going above their head [without ever addressing it with them directly] will *not* open up a valuable discussion, and makes you look like a turd.

4. Volunteer to chaperone. Even if you're "lame" in your kid's eyes. You are just the chaperone another kid needs.

5. Find a reason to celebrate your youth minister/pastor.

Never say, do, or imply anything that makes the youth minister come across as "lesser" than others on the ministry staff. For example, no comments about "Now that you have a kid, are you going to become a real preacher?" Or use of phrases such as "just the youth pastor," etc.

Speaking of having a kid, if your youth pastor's family has child(ren), respect their desire (more accurately, *need*!) for family time.

I second the comment about going above the youth pastor to complain to leadership without first talking to the youth pastor. That action speaks volumes in many ways. None are positive.

Before you contact the youth minister to see what time the devotional will be . . . double-check to make sure the answer isn't in the mass text that was just sent out thirty minutes ago.

Remind them that a youth minister is working for the good of the entire youth ministry; sometimes a specific program or event may not be what they want for their student, but it may be what is best for the ministry as a whole.

Remember to encourage your youth minister.

SAMPLE INTERNSHIP AGREEMENT

Intern: _____ Church: _____

Start Date: _____ End Date: _____

Intern's supervisor / direct report: _____

Compensation: $ _____/week

Other benefits:
- Expenses paid or reimbursed for all youth-related functions
- Travel expenses reimbursed to and from _____

Housing: With church member _____ from _____ until _____

Job expectations:
- Imitate the heart of Christ
- Chaperone all trips
- Maintain office hours of 10:00–2:00 Tuesday–Friday unless meeting with teens; weekly day off will be Monday
- Make contact with inactive members

- Contact all teens who miss Sunday and Wednesday meetings by phone or mail
- Spend time building relationships with girls in their environment
- Organize a weekly outing with a small group of teens, inviting a couple of inactive members to join
- Help prepare / set up and tear down / clean up all events
- Help prepare flyers and other promotional materials
- Plan, prepare, and execute the Middle School Thrill weekend

_____

Intern's Signature   Date

_____

Supervisor's Signature   Date

SAMPLE JOB OFFER LETTER

Dear _____,

It is my pleasure to extend the following offer of employment to you on behalf of _____ Church.

[Here, you would insert one or two encouraging sentences, specific to this person's personality and gifts, and express why you are thrilled to extend this offer to him or her.]

I am attaching your job description, but here are a few specific terms related to the offer that I wanted to make sure were clear:

Your title will be _____ and you will report to _____.

Your annual salary will be $_____, paid in □ biweekly / □ monthly installments of $_____, subject to deductions for taxes and other withholdings as required by law or the policies of our congregation.

Your position will include the following benefits:

- three weeks paid vacation
- one week study leave

Health benefits will be as follows: *[Detail any health insurance policies and who they cover. What percentage of the* *monthly premium will the church pay? Does this include dental and vision?]*

Retirement: *[Detail any 401(k) or 403(b) program and/or matching contributions the church would provide.]*

The church also plans to assist with the cost of your move, up to a total of $_____$.

The youth ministry budget will include a leadership expense line item of $_____$ a year to cover any normal travel, phone, or other expenses occurred in the process of executing the responsibilities of your position.

We look forward to your beginning your first day with us on _____.

[You will want to conclude with one more encouraging sentence that expresses enthusiasm about the new person joining your staff.]

[Include the signature of the clergy person and/or laypersons responsible for hiring and managing the youth director.]

This offer letter, along with the final form of any referenced documents, represents the entire agreement between the church and _____, and no verbal or written agreements, promises, or representations that are not specifically stated in this offer are or will be binding upon our church. If you are in agreement with the above outline, please sign below. This offer will be in effect for five business days.

Signatures:

_____

(Church's Name, Date)

_____

(Candidate's Name, Date)

TWO OBVIOUS REMINDERS

Two things that have been implied or clearly presented in this book: pray and communicate! I know it may seem redundant, but these two items are crucial to establishing a positive and successful relationship with your youth minister.

PRAY

Prayer does things for the one delivering and receiving the prayer. As a parent, praying for your youth minister is asking the Lord to bless someone who will be spending time with your student. What an important focus of time in prayer. As a youth minister, knowing someone is praying for you and your ministry gives great encouragement.

In short, prayer does things:

> He has delivered us from such a deadly peril, and he will deliver us again. On him we have set our hope that he will continue to deliver us, as you help us by your prayers. Then many will give thanks on our behalf for the gracious favor granted us in answer to the prayers of many. (2 Cor. 1:10ff.)

For this reason, ever since I heard about your faith
in the Lord Jesus and your love for all God's people, I
have not stopped giving thanks for you, remember-
ing you in my prayers. I keep asking that the God of
our Lord Jesus Christ, the glorious Father, may give
you the Spirit of wisdom and revelation, so that you
may know him better. (Eph. 1:15ff.)

And pray in the Spirit on all occasions with all kinds
of prayers and requests. With this in mind, be alert
and always keep on praying for all the Lord's people.
(Eph. 6:18)

Do not be anxious about anything, but in every
situation, by prayer and petition, with thanksgiving,
present your requests to God. And the peace of God,
which transcends all understanding, will guard your
hearts and your minds in Christ Jesus. (Phil. 4:6ff.)

Devote yourselves to prayer, being watchful and
thankful. And pray for us, too, that God may open
a door for our message, so that we may proclaim
the mystery of Christ, for which I am in chains.
(Col. 4:2ff.)

Is anyone among you in trouble? Let them pray. Is anyone happy? Let them sing songs of praise. Is anyone
among you sick? Let them call the elders of the church
to pray over them and anoint them with oil in the
name of the Lord. And the prayer offered in faith will
make the sick person well; the Lord will raise them up.
If they have sinned, they will be forgiven. Therefore
confess your sins to each other and pray for each other

so that you may be healed. The prayer of a righteous person is powerful and effective. (James 5:13ff.)

Did you notice all that prayer does for the one speaking and the one receiving the focus of prayer? Your youth ministers are praying for you. Remember to pray for them. Pray for their families, their health, their financial stability, their emotional stability, and so on. Pray for their success in ministry. When they thrive, you and your students can thrive as well.

COMMUNICATE

Talk to your youth ministers. Not just about "youth ministry things"; talk to them often, about several things. This establishes a level of trust and normality for both parents and youth ministers. Your willingness to communicate will encourage your youth ministers more than you know and create a relationship that will make it easier to navigate any difficult conversations about "youth ministry things" and personal and family struggles.

A WORD ON DISAGREEMENTS

We are living in a conflict-rich environment. As such, you should not be shocked when disagreements occur between parents and students, parents and other parents, or parents and youth ministers. We encourage you to go back and read the chapter "Conflict Matters" if you are currently facing such a scenario with your youth minister. We thought it would be helpful to list a few of the more common disagreements we have experienced that, when left unattended or handled poorly, create job-ending outcomes:

- ❀ Your youth minister scheduled an event on top of an already scheduled school event.
- ❀ Your youth minister invited someone from a different denomination to speak to the youth group.
- ❀ Your youth minister has planned an activity with the other church(es) in town.
- ❀ Your youth minister did something different (e.g., chose a new kind of music or a certain video, led worship a certain way, broached gender-leadership inclusion, etc.) during youth worship.

* Your youth minister did not support or even attend an important historical church event.
* Your youth minister does not agree with and is teaching content contrary to your denomination's belief and practice.
* Your youth minister is a bad communicator and organizer (and the budget is in shambles as well).
* Your youth minister does not spend enough time with your student.
* Your youth minister has a different idea of what "effective programming" looks like in youth ministry.

The list could go on, but you get the idea. Some disagreements will be larger than others. Again, disagreements will happen. There is not a perfect youth minister, parent, student, or church, and neither are they always perfectly compatible; we are human. Handling a disagreement productively is essential in keeping a healthy relationship with your youth minister and supporting a growing, vibrant youth ministry.

HIRING AND FIRING RESOURCES

We are blessed to live in a resource-rich youth ministry culture. There are a number of organizations and academic institutions that provide step-by-step guides, consultation services, and even assistance in finding and matching youth ministers with your opportunity. Many, if not all, welcome initial correspondence free of charge. The kind of assistance offered varies by expertise, resources, and cost, but all are trusted partners:

Hope Network (hopenetworkministries.org)

Ministry Architects (www.ministryarchitects.com)

Slingshot Group (www.slingshotgroup.org)

Youth Specialties Job Bank (jobbank.youthspecialties.com)

Great assistance can also be found by contacting the youth ministry professor(s) at your denomination's seminaries, universities, and graduate schools.

NOTES

Preface

[1] The monumental work of the National Study of Youth and Religion (www.youthandreligion.org) and the practical insights offered by the Fuller Youth Institute (www.fulleryouthinstitute.org) and the Barna Institute (www.barna.org) are chief among these resources.

Introduction

[1] Fuller Youth Institute, D6, Orange, and Barna are the leading national organizations looking into this.

[2] The National Study on Youth and Religion's website is www.youthandreligion.org. A book by Christian Smith with Melinda Lundquist Denton, *Soul Searching: The Religious and Spiritual Lives of American Teenagers*, provides a full discussion of this and other truths concerning adolescent spirituality.

Affirmation Matters

[1] In light of Deuteronomy 6:4ff., this is a particularly important affirmation.

Failure Matters

[1] We have most often seen this type of consequence-shielding behavior from church leaders who believe they are helping the youth minister by protecting her from the criticism of parents. Eventually, the youth minister is terminated because the criticism reaches a crescendo that forces the hand of the church leaders. In the end, the youth minister has no clue that there is a problem until it is too late to fix it.

[2] Scott Cormode, "Conflict and Change," lecture, Fuller Seminary, October 2019.

Conflict Matters

[1] Even though avoidance and silence appear to be great solutions to conflict, individuals and organizations that choose those routes are simply pushing their conflict farther down the road, feeding resentment, and adding fuel to the argument that will eventually manifest.

[2] Titus 3:1–11 is an excellent example.

Friendship Matters

[1] Disclaimer: This is not a time to indoctrinate your youth pastor with your vision of youth group while you have them hostage.

Serving Matters

[1] The work of the Barna Research Group (www.barna.com), the Fuller Youth Institute (www.fulleryouthinstitute.com), and the National Study on Youth and Religion (www.youthandreligion.org) substantiate this truth—a truth supported in Deuteronomy 6:4ff.

Partnership Matters

[1] Since Hebrew doesn't have particular singular and plural pronouns, it is possible, and perhaps more accurate, to read the Shema this way: "These commandments that I give you today are to be on your hearts. Impress them on all y'alls children. Talk about them when all y'all sit at home and when y'all walk along the road, when y'all lie down and when y'all get up. Tie them as symbols on all y'alls hands and bind them on y'alls foreheads. Write them on the doorframes of all y'alls houses and on y'alls gates" (Deut. 6:4–9).

[2] As mentioned in a previous chapter, the monumental work of the National Study of Youth and Religion (www.youthandreligion.org) and the practical insights offered by the Fuller Youth Institute (www .fulleryouthinstitute.org) and the Barna Institute (www.barna.org) are chief among these resources.

[3] Again, the National Study of Youth and Religion, the Fuller Youth Institute, and the Barna Institute support this.

[4] This truth is found in Christian Smith with Melinda Lundquist Denton, *Soul Searching: The Religious and Spiritual Lives of American Teenagers* (Oxford: Oxford University Press, 2005).

[5] A great term coined by the Fuller Youth Institute to identify parents who leave all the spiritual formation of their students to the paid, youth ministry professionals.

[6] Reggie Joiner, in *Think Orange* (Colorado Springs, CO: David C. Cook, 2009), points out that the average youth minister gets about fifty

to eighty hours of influence in a year with any given teen while that same teen's parent gets over three thousand hours of influence in the same year. Bottom line, your youth minister cannot "out influence" you (92).

Wisdom Matters

[1] Think how TikTok is simply a rebirth of Vine. Facebook was at one time the new Myspace.

[2] Please do not take this comment to mean that a person with children is more qualified for youth ministry than one who is single. Each stage of life has its own strengths and shortcomings—including as they relate to youth ministry. For example, a single person may have far more availability than a young married couple with a new family, while a couple with a new family may bring more maternal and paternal instincts to a youth ministry than a new college graduate.

[3] No, no you cannot. One must budget at least three to four hours for such a task.

Discipleship Matters

[1] See Christian Smith with Melinda Lundquist Denton, *Soul Searching: The Religious and Spiritual Lives of American Teenagers* (Oxford: Oxford University Press, 2009), 18: "Even though agents of religious socialization do not appear to be wildly successful in fostering clarity and articulacy about faith among teens, it remains true that parents and other adults exert huge influence in the lives of American adolescents—whether for good or ill, and whether adults can perceive it or not—when it comes to religious faith and most other areas of teen's lives."

[2] See Chap Clark, *Hurt 2.0: Inside the World of Today's Teenagers* (Ada, MI: Baker Academic, 2011), 28. He continues, "The young have not arrogantly turned their backs on the adult world. Rather, they have been forced by a personal sense of abandonment to band together and create their own world—separate, semisecret, and vastly different from the world around them."

[3] See Smith with Denton, *Soul Searching*, 117: "In the absence of parental encouragement by example to attend religious services, religious congregations that offer teenagers organized youth groups—particularly those with full-time, paid, adult youth group leaders—seem to make a significant difference in attracting teens to attend congregational religious services. Well-developed, congregational-based youth groups with established youth leaders likely provide teens who lack active parental support appealing doorways into and relational ties encouraging greater religious participation in the life of religious congregations."

Discipline Matters

[1] The purpose of this chapter is to assist parents in supporting discipline in youth ministry; we will not discuss what is and is not appropriate discipline. Rest assured, however, that those conversations happen in our youth group classes, at the seminars where we present, and in our courses for the adults we train for ministry.

[2] I remember leading a trip once where the theme was Sabbath, and one of the things that we were practicing taking a break from was our technology. I asked students to leave their phones either at home or with one of our leaders. I remember vividly one parent telling their teen *not* to turn in her phone and that she didn't have to. It was terribly discouraging to have a parent actively working against discipline.

[3] If clear expectations are not communicated, follow the other suggestions. If you are expecting a conflict, read the chapter "Conflict Matters."

[4] Here is something we parents need to remember. While the discipline is about the student's behavior, parents need to be self-aware so they can identify and/or correct any behaviors and/or parenting deficiencies that may have contributed to the student's misconduct.

Internships Ministry

[1] Heads up! Most churches are skirting labor laws in their states by giving interns a weekly "salary" and asking them to work forty, fifty, or sixty hours, thinking that is fine. You need to check with experts who can give you sound counsel regarding how to best compensate your summer interns legally in your state.

Hiring Matters

[1] Some of the problems: Some candidates interview really well, gather a lot of "votes," and leave and/or are fired quickly. Candidates who are chosen in a close vote with another candidate start their ministry at a disadvantage. Church members who dislike all the candidates put before them feel as if they are choosing the best of the worst; not a great way for a youth minister to begin a ministry.

[2] This mindset focus and programmatic shift can be found in the Sticky Faith (https://fulleryouthinstitute.org/stickyfaith) and Growing Young (https://fulleryouthinstitute.org/growingyoung) research conducted by the Fuller Youth Institute.

[1] This is a difficult thing to say to a terminated youth minister. If you are contacted by another church concerning the terminated youth minister, and

you find it prudent and/or are legally prevented from sharing confidential information, you can simply say, "We could not hire them to work at our church" as a response.

Money Matters

[1] There has yet to be significant research to confirm this fact. In our anecdotal experience, there seems to be merit in this worth considering.

[2] The average size of a church in the United States hovers at about 150 members according to the most reliable research.

[3] Try googling the name of your local school district and "teacher pay scales."

Sabbath Matters

[1] Adele Ahlberg Calhoun, *Spiritual Disciplines Handbook: Practices That Transform Us* (Downers Grove, IL: InterVarsity Press, 2015), 42.

[2] James Bryan Smith, *The Good and Beautiful God: Falling in Love with the God Jesus Knows* (Downers Grove, IL: InterVarsity Press, 2009), 33.

[3] Barbara Brown Taylor, *An Altar in the World: Finding the Sacred beneath Our Feet* (Norwich, UK: Canterbury Press, 2017), 130.

ABOUT THE AUTHORS

With more than fifty years of combined experience in youth ministry, we have served as full-time youth ministers in the context of local churches. We have been parents of teenage sons and daughters in youth ministry. We have served as volunteers, we have served as elders, and we currently teach youth ministry to the next generation of leaders at the university level. Our careers and our passions exist at the intersection of adolescent faith development and healthy church community. We know how important youth ministry is for the church and how important church is for youth ministry. We also know that neither ministry can be effective without the other.

DR. DAVID FRAZE

Dr. David Fraze is the James A. Buddy Davidson Endowed Chair of Youth & Family Ministry at Lubbock Christian University. He has served over twenty years working with adolescents as a full-time youth minister (at Green Lawn Church of Christ in Lubbock, Texas, and the Hills Church in North Richland Hills, Texas) and eleven years working with adolescents in part-time church and parachurch organizations.

Fraze currently serves as a youth ministry volunteer with the Monterey Church of Christ in Lubbock, Texas. He works with athletes across the state and is a character coach for the Frenship football program. He also works with the Fuller Youth Institute and Youth Specialties to train and equip youth workers, parents, and church leaders. He is a coach with the Dallas Cowboys Football Youth Academy. He also writes and is the personality for a weekly TV segment on KCBD NewsChannel 11 called "That's Good Stuff."

Fraze holds three theological degrees: two from Lubbock Christian University in Lubbock, Texas; a BA and MA in biblical studies; and a DMin in youth and family ministry from Fuller Theological Seminary in Pasadena, California. He also completed an MDiv equivalency and was an adjunct professor at Abilene Christian University in Abilene, Texas.

Fraze lives in Lubbock, Texas, with his wife, Lisa, and daughter, Shelbee. His son, Braeden, and daughter-in-law, Jenna, live in Andrews, Texas, and are expecting their first child.

DR. WALTER SURDACKI

Dr. Walter Surdacki has served as professor of youth and family ministry at Lipscomb University since 2008. Surdacki spent over sixteen years working with adolescents as a full-time youth minister in local churches in California (Torrance Church of Christ, Malibu Church of Christ, and Campbell Church of Christ).

Surdacki served as a youth ministry volunteer before and during his daughters' teen years. He currently serves as an elder for his church in the Nashville, Tennessee, area.

Surdacki holds four theology degrees: a BA in biblical studies from the Austin Graduate School of Theology in Austin, Texas; an MS in ministry from Pepperdine University in Malibu, California; and both an MDiv and a DMin in youth and family ministry from Fuller Theological Seminary in Pasadena, California.